entertaining simple

MATTHEW MEAD

Photographs by Quentin Bacon / Text with Jill Kirchner Simpson

JOHN WILEY & SONS, INC.

WILEY

Published by John Wiley & Sons, Inc., Hoboken, New Jersey

Published simultaneously in Canada

For general information on our other products and services or for technical support, please contact our Customer Care Department within the United States at (877) 762-2974, outside the United States at (317) 572-3993 or fax (317) 572-4002.

Wiley also publishes its books in a variety of electronic formats. Some content that appears in print may not be available in electronic books. For more information about Wiley products, visit our web site at www.wiley.com.

Library of Congress Cataloging-in-Publication Data:

Mead, Matthew.
 Entertaining simple custom / Matthew Mead ; text with Jill Kircher
Simpson ; photography by Quentin Bacon.
      p. cm.
 Includes index.
 ISBN 978-0-470-55594-1 (pbk.)
 1. Entertaining. 2. Cookery. 3. Tableware. I. Kirchner, Jill. II.
Title.
 TX731.M3968 2009
 642'.4—dc22

                            2009025992

Printed in the United States of America
10 9 8 7 6 5 4 3 2 1

To Jenny and my amazing creative team,
Lisa Renauld and Lisa Bisson,
for how we have entertained each other...
and to Quentin for his beautiful images
and unparalleled style.

contents

1

the entertaining simple pantry

essential elements,
storage, and display

2

simple get-togethers

index

acknowledgments

Entertaining is fun... and I can't thank my friends and family enough for contributing to all the great times we share together. Thank you to my wife, Jenny, and our daughters, who are always supportive and insightful and help with testing and tasting my recipes and giving me feedback.

My assistants, Lisa Renauld and Lisa Bisson, who do a great deal of the hard work and always make me think about the ease and availability of ingredients and supplies for each and every project.

Quentin Bacon for the best and most beautiful photographs; they are so colorful and engaging.

Jill Kirchner Simpson, who helps me to say what I want in a thoughtful and precise way.

Doug Turshen for his exceptional and beautiful design of this book.

My agent, Colleen Mohyde, and the Doe Coover Agency, who receive all my ideas with excitement and enthusiasm.

My culinary advisers, Samantha French and Sue Chandler, who take on each challenge with vim and vigor, and Cynthia Crockett of Bakery 42, who has a certain way with bread.

My fabrication team, Mary and Gordon Welch and Woody Roberts, who complete all my projects at a moment's notice.

To my friends in the style community, especially Carol Sheehan, Mary Emmerling, Gayle Butler, Kelly Kegans, and Trish Foley.

To all the guests at our parties, too many to list but extremely appreciated. Especially Lisa Renauld's extended family and Jenny's nieces and nephews as well as their spouses—thank you so much.

To Justin Schwartz and everyone at John Wiley & Sons. Thank you for recognizing our brand and perpetuating it in such a thoughtful and enduring way.

To my ultimate support team: Barry Costa and his brilliant web design; Carol Spier for keeping my recipes fresh and correct; my sister, Ann Ash, who is always there with editorial support in so many ways; and my parents, without whose love and support this would not be possible... THANK YOU.

1

the entertaining simple pantry
essential elements, storage, and display

The foundation of the Entertaining Simple approach is a core "wardrobe" of tableware—white ceramic plates and bowls, clear glasses, simple serving pieces—that can be adapted for a wide variety of uses, from casual brunches to dress-up dinners. The fact is, many of us actually own much more than this core wardrobe, and it is a challenge to weed out what you don't really need. To help, I have used my years of experience entertaining and styling food photography for magazines, to come up with a list of the recommended basics (see "The Entertaining Simple Pantry," starting on page 28). These basics are all that you'll need to entertain in any setting. This doesn't mean you have to throw everything else away, but you should give storage priority to your "essentials" and keep things that you don't rely on regularly in a more remote location.

The first step is to focus on all-white and clear glass items; this gives you a surprisingly wide range of options, as well as a unifying theme. You can add in old, new, or handed-down pieces and they will all work together. White and glass also give a pleasing sense of visual order. When everything is the same color, the

All-white and clear glass items give you a surprisingly

different shapes and silhouettes come to the fore. White porcelain and glass have been tableware classics for centuries because they meld seamlessly with almost any design scheme, from the most traditional, elegant interiors to more rustic homes to very modern spaces.

The next step is to create a well-organized area to store and access your entertaining basics. Whether you live in an apartment, cottage, or house, there are options that can work well for any amount of space. I have found, in general, that open or glass-fronted storage, where you can see what you need and get to it easily, often works best. You're more likely to use things when you see them every day. It also streamlines preparation, so you don't have to dig through dark cupboards, get out a stepladder to reach high shelves, or tramp down to the basement to find what you need. And because the Entertaining Simple pantry has been pared down to the essentials, it doesn't require a great deal of space. By weeding out the pieces you don't use very often—the fondue set, the margarita glasses, the painted pottery bought on vacation, the fine cut-crystal goblets—and homing in on a basic wardrobe that can be used for everyday meals as well as special occasions, you'll have less to store and it will be easier to organize.

A "pantry" can be anything from a kitchen cabinet to a freestanding china cupboard

wide range of options

to a rolling cart. You can create one in a little-used closet or even in a tool chest. I drew on the idea of a modern-day butler's pantry when I designed the kitchen for my photo studio. Instead of a separate closet or pantry, however, I carved out space in a corner of the room for custom-built storage cupboards that are nearly floor-to-ceiling. They are fitted with shelves and doors that have glass panels on top to show off shapely ceramic and glass pieces, and are solid wood on the bottom to conceal more utilitarian storage, such as wine bottles, linens, and candles. The shelves hold easy-to-access stacks of plates, platters, bowls, and serving pieces in white, with pieces of clear glass mixed in to create a pleasing display. What I love about this storage solution is that when the doors are open, I have full view of everything I need for a gathering and can easily pull it out to set the table or organize the buffet in a matter of minutes. I also placed deep, open shelves above my cooktop for my most frequently used serving pieces, which makes it easier to arrange and

You're more likely to use things

serve food right from the pan.

When space is more limited, there are plenty of other creative options. Open shelves, if arranged neatly, create a form of wall art in the dining room or kitchen (even living room) and don't take up valuable floor or counter space. Small storage islands or bar carts on wheels offer portability, a boon in cramped quarters. When my wife, Jenny, and I were first married, we had a small apartment with very little storage space. The kitchen cabinets were tiny and dark and offered only enough room for canned goods and dry ingredients. Our solution was a rolling cart with shelves that could be moved easily from kitchen to dining room as needed. It worked out beautifully, as its butcher block top also supplemented the limited counter and workspace.

In our first house, where we had slightly more room, we had the walls of our dining room outfitted with bracketed shelves, which held everything we needed within steps of the dining area, so it was easy for even the children to set the table. Whatever option you choose based on your space and aesthetic preferences, having a well-edited and well-organized pantry is key.

when you see them every day

the entertaining simple pantry

Over the years, these are the items that I have found to be the most useful for entertaining. This collection is the foundation for all the ideas and parties you will see in the chapters that follow. Of course, you can substitute or add the things you yourself like best and have come to rely on, but consider this a general guide to a well-equipped but not over-stuffed wardrobe for entertaining as well as everyday living. This list can also serve as an excellent checklist for a wedding or housewarming registry or for anyone starting out on their own.

The beauty of these items is that they are easy to find almost anywhere—simple white ceramic and glass basics are sold at many retailers nationwide (and online) including Crate & Barrel, Pottery Barn, IKEA, Target, Williams-Sonoma, and more. Even the less familiar items such as eggcups can be found at places such as Crate & Barrel and Sur La Table. The only tricky item to track down might be a celery vase (vintage pieces are easier to find—try eBay) but you can substitute glasses in a similar shape. And whether you find these pieces old or new, secondhand or separated from a set, the white and clear palette unifies them all easily. Please note: The sizes listed are just a general suggestion; you should by no means feel limited to them.

Core Items

12	place settings including dinner plates, salad/dessert plates, and bowls
12	glass tumblers
12	wine glasses
12	coffee cups/handleless mugs
12	place settings of flatware including salad forks, dinner forks, knives, and spoons
1–2	large platters
1	set nesting mixing bowls
6–12	votive holders
1	tablecloth
12	napkins

Serving Utensils

2–3	large serving spoons, set of salad servers, carving knife and fork, ladle, cheese knife

Add Next

1	glass pitcher
1	ice bucket and tongs
1	set of bar tools (ice crusher, jigger, strainer, mixing spoon, drink stirrers, bottle opener)
1	or more cake stands and/or compotes
2	or more glass cylinders
	Large oval and rectangular ceramic baking dishes

Optional

12	hors d'oeuvres plates (four-inch diameter)
18	cocktail napkins
12	glass salad plates
	Small oval bowls
	Glass handleless mugs
	Coffee- and teapots
	Cruets
	Decanter
	Napkin rings
	Egg cups
	Celery vases
	Glass bottles

sizes and details

DINNER PLATES

The dinner plate is a classic that offers a great deal of versatility. Place a clear salad plate on top and it becomes a charger. Layer smaller bowls on top and it becomes a tray. Serve a roasted chicken or a cake on it and it becomes a platter.

Size: 10–11 inches diameter

SALAD PLATES

A salad plate is also the perfect size for dessert, breakfast, lunch, appetizers, or children's plates—any time you don't need quite such a large plate. It also offers endless opportunities for layering with dinner plates. **Size:** 8–9 inches diameter

BOWLS

Bowls go from cereal in the morning to salad or noodles at lunch to ice cream at night. They are so useful, you may even want more than twelve. You could also float a lush blossom in one or create a centerpiece by placing a chunky candle in the center. **Size:** 7–9 inches diameter

GLASS TUMBLERS

Clear tumblers can be used to serve everything from chocolate milk to sauvignon blanc to ice cream parfaits. I like the oversize ones that are made of very thin glass. **Size:** 5 inches tall (approximately 16 ounces)

WINE GLASSES

Medium-size balloon glasses are perfect for red wine, or they can display an elegant dessert, a floating candle centerpiece, or serve as a table favor filled with chocolate truffles. **Size:** 7 inches tall; 3-inch diameter (approximately 16 ounces)

HANDLELESS MUGS

I have always been a big fan of the handleless mug. There is nothing more comforting than wrapping your hands around a hot mug of soup or cocoa on a cold day or clasping an icy drink on a hot summer day. They are also sleek vessels for serving or showing off tall items like breadsticks or flowers.

Size: 4 1/2 inches tall (approximately 16 ounces)

SMALL OVAL BOWLS

A small oval bowl is more unusual than a round one, and especially useful for offering a single serving of everything from spiced nuts to condiments to potatoes. Fill these bowls with toppings for an ice cream sundae bar or with cut fruit and cubes of pound cake for a dessert fondue.

Size: 4 1/2 inches diameter

NESTING MIXING BOWLS

I like items that nest because they store so compactly, but I also like graduated mixing bowls because they can be used for so many things beyond mixing. Fill the large one with ice and nest a smaller one inside to keep salads, frozen treats, and dips cold; or use them for dip and chips; or fill with fresh fruits for a centerpiece. These can be found very inexpensively in sets and you will use them constantly.

Size: 10 1/2 inches diameter x 6 inches tall; 8 inches diameter x 4 1/2 inches tall; and 6 inches diameter x 3 1/4 inches tall

ICE BUCKET

A necessity for any bar or when serving beverages for a group, a glass ice bucket can also hold a beautiful flower arrangement, or silverware for an informal buffet.

CANDLES

I keep dripless white and/or cream unscented candles on hand at all times. I use tapers, votives, tea lights, and pillars in an array of sizes. Store candles in a cool, dry place. You can buy sticky wax buttons to help secure taper candles inside candlesticks.

PLATTERS

I have collected platters for years and regard them as some of the most important pieces in my pantry. Platters corral ingredients as I move them from refrigerator to workspace, show off fresh produce, and proudly offer the meal at the table. **Sizes:** 18 and 13 inches long

GLASS VOTIVES

These are essential for candlelight at the table, but offer many other uses as well. After dinner they make the perfect small espresso cup; or use them for serving condiments and sauces, or even sake or liqueurs. **Size:** 2 1/2 inches tall x 3 inches diameter

NAPKINS

I prefer white because it goes with everything
and creates a clean backdrop for sprigs of
herbs, flowers, or colorful name tags. Square
cocktail napkins with a simple hemstitch
are a nice accompaniment for drinks.
Twelve generous-size dinner napkins with
hemstitching are always nice to have on hand.
Sizes: 6-inch square, 10-inch square, and
20-inch square

PORCELAIN OR METAL NAPKIN RINGS

Whether you collect old silver rings or new
ironstone ones, they are the perfect way
to cinch a napkin. Keep them simple or add
embellishments (see Chapter 3).

GLASS CYLINDER AND GLASS BOTTLES

Recycle glass wine and soda bottles for a variety of uses. Fill with cocktails or fruit juice and a straw, or with syrup for pancakes. Group bottles together and place single stems of flowers in each for an intriguing centerpiece. I use glass cylinders for all types of foods and centerpieces. **Bottle Size:** 7 inches tall (8 ounces). **Cylinder Size:** 7 inches tall x 9 inches diameter

EGGCUPS

Eggcups are the perfect way to serve soft-boiled eggs, but also individual portions of maple syrup, after-dinner mints, or a small bouquet for each guest.

HORS D'OEUVRES PLATES AND BOWLS

These plates and bowls can be used together or apart, to hold perfect individual portions of appetizers or desserts. **Plate Size:** 5 inches diameter round **Bowl Size:** 2 inches tall x 3 1/2 inches diameter (1/2 cup)

GLASS PLATES

Chameleons of the table, these stylish plates add a layer of sparkle at each place setting and can take on different looks with the addition of patterned papers, pressed botanicals, monograms, or old pieces of linen and lace. **Size:** Dessert/salad plate, 8 inches diameter

CAKE STAND, COMPOTE, AND CELERY VASES

These pieces are a wonderful way to show off whatever you choose to serve in them. Their pedestal bases make them perfect for a sideboard or buffet because they add verticality to the display and leave more table space for other dishes.

The perfect way to give food the spotlight, a cake stand literally puts it "on a pedestal." It elevates items in height as well as importance. Cake stands can be used for anything from crackers and cheese to a show-stopping dessert.

The compote is sister to the cake stand, providing the same kind of showcase for fruits, flowers, or desserts that have a sauce or liquid component. A compote can be used as a centerpiece for the table, or on a buffet to hold bundles of silverware, or filled with a cold yogurt fruit dip and surrounded with skewered fruit.

Celery vases were originally designed, as their name implies, to hold celery. You can use them to give a wide array of foods—crackers, candy, nuts, crudités—more of a presence on the table. Or fill with bread sticks for an appetizer tray or lollipops for a kids' party.

popovers

It's always magic to see the runny batter puff into a lovely, hollow pastry that's crisp on the outside and soft on the inside.

- **3½ cups whole milk or half-and-half**
- **4 cups bread flour**
- **1½ teaspoons salt**
- **1 teaspoon baking powder**
- **6 large eggs, at room temperature**
- **4 tablespoons (¼ cup) unsalted butter, melted**
- **Butter for serving**

1. Preheat the oven to 450°F.

2. Microwave the milk for approximately 1½ minutes, or until the milk is warm to the touch. Spoon the flour into a cup and scrape a knife across the top to level it (do not shake the cup to settle the flour). Sift the flour, salt, and baking powder together into a large bowl.

3. In a blender, process the eggs, milk, and melted butter for approximately 10 seconds, until blended. Add the flour mixture to the egg mixture in the blender. Process 10 to 15 seconds or until just combined; the batter should be a bit lumpy. Let rest at room temperature for one hour.

4. Divide the batter evenly among 8 glass baking cups, filling them almost to the top. Bake for 15 minutes; do not open the oven door. Reduce the oven temperature to 375°F. Bake the popovers for 20 to 25 minutes more or until they are deep golden brown on the outside and airy on the inside. (Under-baking can cause popovers to collapse after they're removed from the oven.) Remove the popovers from the oven, and turn out onto a wire rack. Pierce the side of each popover with the tip of a small sharp knife to let the steam escape. Serve immediately with lots of butter.

Serves 8

GLASS MUGS

Clear glass reveals whatever's inside, making it even prettier and more appealing. Glass mugs are often ovenproof and great for baking as well as for showing off a frothy latte or layered dessert.

Size: 3 1/2 inches tall (approximately 8 ounces)

let each piece multi-task for you

HANDLELESS PITCHER AND CRUETS

All types of sauces and dressings—gravy, vinaigrette, molé, even barbecue sauce, look nicer on the table and are more easily poured in these vessels. **Handleless Pitcher/Size:** 8 inches tall **Small Cruet/Size:** 3 inches tall **Large Cruet/Size:** 4 1/2 inches tall

TEAPOT AND COFFEEPOT

Not just for coffee and tea—use them to serve all kinds of hot liquids like hot buttered rum, hot chocolate, or even mulled wine and cider. I use a teapot in the summer to water herb plants in my centerpiece or even to hold a bouquet.

GLASS PITCHER AND DECANTER

A clear glass pitcher and decanter serve beverages with simple elegance. Add colorful fruits (fresh or frozen into ice) or edible flowers and herbs for drama. Or use them to hold a striking arrangement. **Glass Pitcher Size:** 8–12 inches tall (10 cups) **Decanter Size:** 14 inches tall (10 cups)

BAKING DISHES

Unlike platters, baking dishes have sides, making them useful not only for baking foods, but also as serving trays. **Baking Dish Sizes:** 10 inches wide x 18 inches long and 8 inches wide x 15 inches long

SERVING PIECES

Serving pieces are the most public face of your flatware—
what is shown off on the table—so be sure to have an
assortment of serving spoons and forks, a carving set,
and salad servers. You might want to add a ladle, pie/cake
server, and a bar set—ice tongs, a jigger, a strainer, stirrers,
a bottle opener, and a bar knife.

2

simple get-togethers

The Entertaining Simple approach to hosting gives you the chance to gather with friends or family, toast a special occasion, or just enjoy being together, without a lot of fuss and formality—an opportunity to actually enjoy your own parties, instead of slaving away behind the scenes. Choosing a fun theme or appealing look for a party creates an organizing principle and gives you the spark of inspiration and motivation to guide your ideas and choices. In the next two chapters, you'll find lots of creative ideas, along with complete party guides to help you put it all together, including menus, recipes, decorating ideas, how-tos, and serving tips. Don't feel you need to follow any one of these plans "by the book"; instead, pick and choose what you like and what works best for your own event, adding, subtracting, or swapping recipes and elements as desired.

Keep in mind that in every case, you can make things even simpler by buying some or many of the dishes ready-made, depending on what's available near you. Get to know which food shops or take-out restaurants offer great roasted chicken, sumptuous desserts, terrific muffins, or delicious side dishes. Then choose from among the recipes and menus here to decide what things you'd like to make yourself—and keep in mind that many can be made ahead. Most of the recipes also come with invaluable

Choosing a fun theme will help

shortcuts for when you're pressed for time.

The main point is to take a guilt-free approach to entertaining. You don't need to devote hours to creating an elaborate dessert when the pastry shop in town sells wonderful tarts, or make beef Wellington when your guests would equally enjoy a simple roasted chicken. The secret to a great party is to have everything ready, and to be relaxed and engaged enough to participate in the event, introducing guests who don't know one another, breaking the ice, and joining in the conversations. If you are frantically running around, or sequestered in the kitchen for the first half of the party, chances are that anxiety will set the tone for your gathering. Think back to parties you have enjoyed at other people's houses: Was it the fanciness of the food or the fun of the evening that made it memorable? The best way for your guests to have a good time is for you to have one, too!

While the Entertaining Simple approach encourages you to be more relaxed, ironically the best way to do that is with thorough preparation, so you avoid last-minute surprises and chaos. Read through the recipes well ahead of time, make lists of every-thing you need, and do as much as you possibly can in advance: Shop for nonperish-ables early with your regular grocery order. Make or buy decorative elements the week before, and set the table a day in advance if possible. Make ahead (and even freeze) whatever dishes you can.

It can also be a huge help to have extra hands on the day of the actual event. You should not try to do it all on your own. If your spouse or roommate is all thumbs, you can still find plenty of simple jobs and preparations for him or her to do. Children can be surprisingly good helpers when focused on simple tasks—or if they're not, make a play date for them or hire a babysitter to keep them out of your hair. Ask a good friend or family member to come a little early and help with last-minute setup. And if it's a big

guide your menu and choices

party, consider hiring someone to serve, clean up, and/or tend bar. Local colleges and high schools can be a good source of reasonably priced help.

One final consideration for reluctant entertainers: You may need to redefine how you think of entertaining. If the point is to be able to see friends who are in from out of town, or have a last-minute get-together with another family, there is nothing wrong with dressing up take-out food and making it an easy, totally unpressured evening. A great gathering doesn't necessarily have to be a gourmet dinner party either; it could be a pajama-clad brunch, a gab-fest afternoon tea, an outdoor picnic, or a lazy Sunday afternoon kaffeeklatsch. I hope the ideas that follow will inspire you, but please don't let them limit you—the possibilities are almost endless. Think about the events you already enjoy: Conjure up a gourmet pizza party to watch the Oscars; a fajita buffet with margaritas on Cinco de Mayo; a red-white-and-blue brunch for local parade-watchers on the Fourth of July or Memorial Day; or a mint julep cocktail party in honor of the Kentucky Derby. All it takes is that little spark of excitement, and you're off!

family fusion

It doesn't have to be Sunday, of course. Any time you can gather family or friends together around the table for a relaxed, convivial dinner is a special occasion. A classic, soul-satisfying meal of roasted chicken is given an update with fresh herbs and a visually appealing presentation. The menu is designed to appeal to kids and grandparents alike. To simplify your efforts, buy fresh-baked bread and dessert.

menu

HERB-ROASTED CHICKEN

ROASTED ROOT VEGETABLES

TWICE-BAKED POTATO BOATS

ROSEMARY MINI BREADS

**FRESH BERRY
AND CUSTARD GALETTE**

the setting

Gathering around a table, traditionally in the dining room, encourages conversation, but you could make the meal more casual or less expected by serving at a kitchen island, around a family room coffee table, or on a farm table set up outdoors or by the living room fire.

Decant the wine so it can "breathe," and for a cleaner, more modern presentation. Classic comfort food, opposite—roasted chicken and twice-baked potatoes— is always appealing.

The herbs infuse not only the taste of the meal, but the aroma and aesthetics of the table as well. Tuck a sprig of fragrant fresh herbs such as rosemary, lemon verbena, or marjoram in the napkin ring at each place setting.

For an all-natural, unexpected centerpiece, use the oval ceramic baker as a tray, and arrange a landscape of tumblers, bottles, and votives filled with herbs such as flowering chives, sage, oregano, thyme, and marjoram. Add clusters of different kinds of onions around the base. Extend the natural theme by placing color photocopies of images such as feathers or botanicals beneath glass salad plates. The simplicity of the glass and ceramic serving pieces lets the rich colors of the roasted vegetables and berry galette stand out. Optional accent: Use the individual rosemary breads as place card holders. Insert a wire note holder in the top of each loaf and add a place card.

the recipes

herb-roasted chicken

This is a simple recipe that will fill your home with the aroma of fresh herbs.

16 fresh asparagus spears
8   slices bacon, cut in half crosswise
1   whole chicken (3 pounds)
2   teaspoons onion powder
2   tablespoons kosher salt
½   teaspoon freshly ground black pepper
6   tablespoons (¾ stick) unsalted butter, softened
⅓   cup finely chopped fresh oregano
⅓   cup finely chopped fresh parsley
4   tablespoons snipped fresh chives
2   tablespoons finely minced garlic
2   celery stalks, cut in half crosswise

1. Preheat the oven to 350°F.

2. Snap off and discard the woody base from the asparagus spears; if desired, scrape the scales from the stalks. One at a time, cut each spear lengthwise in half and then into 3-inch lengths. Wrap each piece of asparagus with a half strip of bacon and arrange along the inside perimeter of a roasting pan.

3. Sprinkle the chicken inside and out with the onion powder, 1 tablespoon of the salt, and the pepper; place in the roasting pan.

4. In a medium bowl, mix the butter, oregano, parsley, chives, garlic, and remaining 1 tablespoon of the salt, to make a paste. Place 3 tablespoons of the butter mixture in the chicken cavity. Add the celery to the chicken cavity. Dollop the remaining butter on and around the chicken. Bake uncovered for 1 hour and 15 minutes, until an instant-read thermometer inserted in the thigh reads 180°F.

5. Remove the pan from oven and baste the chicken with the drippings. Cover with aluminum foil, and allow to rest at room temperature for about 30 minutes. To serve, transfer the chicken to a platter, arrange the asparagus around the perimeter, and stuff the cavity with fresh parsley.

Serves 4

Simplify: Purchase a rotisserie chicken from the supermarket; serve with steamed asparagus spears sprinkled with crumbled cooked bacon and fresh herbs.

Garnish the roasted chicken with additional fresh herbs, such as Italian parsley, and the asparagus spears wrapped in bacon, which have been used to flavor the chicken.

roasted root vegetables

Roasting this mix of vegetables gives them delicious, intense flavor; I think they're the ultimate comfort food.

- 1 **pound Yukon gold potatoes, scrubbed and cut into 1-inch pieces**
- 1 **pound carrots, peeled and cut into 1-inch pieces**
- 1 **pound parsnips, peeled and cut into 1-inch pieces**
- 1 **pound beets, peeled and cut into 1-inch pieces**
- 2 **onions, peeled and cut into 1-inch pieces**
- 2 **leeks, white and pale green parts, cut into 1-inch-thick rounds**
- 2 **medium zucchini, washed and cut into ½-inch pieces**
- 2 **tablespoons chopped fresh rosemary**
- ½ **cup olive oil**
- 1 **tablespoon salt**
- ½ **teaspoon freshly ground black pepper**
- 10 **cloves garlic, peeled**

1. Preheat the oven to 400°F.

2. In a large roasting pan, place the potatoes, carrots, parsnips, beets, onions, leeks, zucchini, and rosemary. Pour the olive oil over the vegetables and toss to coat. Sprinkle with salt and pepper.

3. Roast for 30 minutes, stirring twice with a wooden spoon. Add the garlic and continue roasting 45 minutes more, until the vegetables are tender when pricked with a fork. Let the vegetables rest at room temperature for 20 minutes; serve warm.

Serves 10

Simplify: Purchase roasted vegetables at a gourmet take-out or grocery store with steam table; reheat at 450°F for 10 to 12 minutes.

Roasted root vegetables, such as butternut squash, parsnips, beets, zucchini, carrots, and onions create a beautiful medley of fall colors, and couldn't be easier—cook right in the rectangular or oval baker for oven-to-table ease.

twice-baked potato boats

I enjoyed making potato boats for Sunday dinner as a kid. To create a delicious crunchy surface, place the filling in individual bowls and brush with melted butter before baking.

12	small Yukon gold potatoes (about 3 pounds), scrubbed
6	large egg yolks
6	tablespoons (¾ stick) unsalted butter, softened
½	cup heavy cream
4	ounces Gruyère cheese, grated (1 cup)
1	tablespoon plus 2 teaspoons kosher salt
¼	teaspoon freshly ground black pepper
4	tablespoons (½ stick) unsalted butter, melted

1. Preheat the oven to 425°F.

2. Wrap each potato in aluminum foil and bake for 1 hour, or until softened. Remove from the oven and unwrap. Lower the oven temperature to 400°F. Let the potatoes cool.

3. Cut each potato in half. Scoop out the flesh into a medium bowl; discard the skins. Mash by hand with a potato masher or wooden spoon. Stir in the egg yolks, 4 tablespoons softened butter, cream, Gruyère, salt, and pepper.

4. Butter 8 ramekins or other small ovenproof bowls with the remaining 2 tablespoons softened butter. Scoop the potato mixture into the ramekins, dividing equally.

5. Place the ramekins on a baking sheet and brush the top of the potato mixture with the 4 tablespoons melted butter. Bake until the top is golden brown and crunchy and the potatoes are set, about 25 minutes. Serve immediately.

Serves 8

Note: This recipe may be prepared ahead through step 4. Cover the filled ramekins with foil and refrigerate up to 1 day ahead of time. When ready to serve, preheat the oven to 400°F and continue with step 5.

Simplify: Purchase freshly baked potatoes from the deli counter or steam table at the grocery store; proceed to step 3 of the recipe.

Rich twice-baked potatoes are baked in individual oval bowls or "boats" for a more special presentation. Cooking foods in individual portions makes them easier to serve and for guests to help themselves.

rosemary mini breads

For a fresh twist on bread with dinner, make these in individual cups for each person.

- 5 cups all-purpose flour
- 1¼ cups water, room temperature
- 2¼ tablespoons kosher salt
- 1 tablespoon active dry yeast
- 1 cup pitted, fresh or jarred kalamata, niçoise, or California olives (reserve 1 to 2 tablespoons of olive brine)
- 1 tablespoon roughly chopped fresh rosemary
- 1 tablespoon olive oil
  Sprigs of fresh rosemary

1. In the bowl of an electric mixer fitted with a dough hook, combine the flour, water, 1¼ tablespoons of the salt, and yeast. Mix on first speed for about 1½ minutes until just combined; mix on second speed for another 1½ minutes until combined—do not overmix. Add the olives, rosemary, and 1 tablespoon of the reserved olive brine; mix until just evenly incorporated. If the dough seems dry and shaggy, add the remaining tablespoon of reserved olive brine and lightly mix until the dough comes together. (Note: To mix by hand, in the bottom of a large bowl, stir together the yeast and water; stir in the salt; add in the flour one cup at a time until mixed; then add in the remaining ingredients, stirring as much as possible. Turn the dough onto lightly floured board and gently knead for about 5 minutes until the dough is thoroughly combined. Return to step 2.)

2. Place the dough into a clean bowl, cover with a damp towel or plastic wrap, and let rise in a warm (not hot) place until doubled, about 1 to 1½ hours.

3. Turn the dough out onto a very lightly floured surface and lightly shape into a round—do not knead. Let rest for 5 minutes. Lightly butter 6 oven-safe baking cups or handleless mugs that hold approximately 2 cups.

4. Divide the dough into 6 pieces. Lightly shape into rounds and drop into the baking cups. Cover and let rise for 45 minutes to 1 hour, or until the dough is just below the surface of the baking cups.

5. Preheat the oven to 400°F.

6. Bake the breads for 35 to 40 minutes, until the tops are golden brown and hardened. Remove from the oven and let cool in the baking cups.

7. Garnish the top of each loaf with a brush of olive oil. Sprinkle with remaining 1 tablespoon of salt and dress with the sprig of fresh rosemary. Serve at each place setting in the baking cup.

Makes 6 mini breads

Note: You can divide the dough into smaller amounts to make rolls and bake in small, buttered ramekins; or divide into larger amounts for 2 regular-size loaves. Adjust the baking times: less for rolls, more for loaves.

Simplify: Add olives and rosemary to a premade baking mix to save time in assembling the dough.

Individual rosemary breads are baked inside the handleless cups. Dust with salt and a sprig of rosemary, and tie natural rickrack around the cup if desired.

fresh berry and custard gallette

This rustic tart has a freeform pie shell that's baked on a baking sheet, not in a pie pan. It's filled with vanilla pudding and fresh berries. Easy, flavorful, and pretty to boot.

PASTRY CRUST

2½	cups all-purpose flour
1	teaspoon salt
1	teaspoon sugar (optional)
1	cup (2 sticks) cold, unsalted butter, cut into small pieces

¼ to ½ cup ice water

FILLING

3	cups prepared vanilla pudding
1	cup sliced, hulled strawberries
½	pint blueberries
½	pint raspberries
½	pint blackberries
1	tablespoon edible lavender flowers or fresh mint blossoms (from your garden, local farmers' market, or gourmet shop)

1. Prepare the crust: In the bowl of a food processor, combine the flour, salt, and sugar, if using. Add the butter and process for about 10 seconds, or until the mixture starts to resemble coarse crumbs. With the processor running, add the ice water by teaspoonfuls through the feed tube until the pastry just holds together without being wet or sticky. If it is crumbly, add a bit more water. (Note: To mix the crust by hand, use a pastry blender or 2 table knives to cut the butter into the flour mixture. Use a fork to gradually blend in the water.)

2. Turn the pastry out onto a large piece of plastic wrap. Use the ends of the plastic wrap to press the pastry into a flat circle with your hands. This makes rolling easier than if the pastry is chilled as a ball. Wrap pastry in the plastic wrap and refrigerate at least 1 hour.

3. Preheat the oven to 375°F. Line a baking sheet with parchment paper.

4. On a floured surface, roll out the pastry to ¼-inch thickness, shaping it into an irregular round about 10 inches across. With your fingers, crimp the edge all around to create a rim (like a pizza). Transfer the pastry to the prepared baking sheet and bake for 20 to 25 minutes. Let the pastry cool completely on a wire rack.

5. Prepare the filling: Spread the pudding into the cooled pastry. In a medium bowl, mix together all of the berries, then spread them over the pudding. Sprinkle the lavender flowers on top and serve.

Serves 8

Simplify: Use ready-made pie crust from the grocery store's freezer case and bake according to package directions.

Dessert is as easy as pie ... or a galette. Shape pie crust into a rounded tart and fold in sides. Brush with butter, bake, and then fill with custard and fresh berries. Serve on a cake stand or compote.

lazy day brunch

You can't beat brunch for casual gatherings. It is perfect for when family or friends are visiting from out of town; to wrap up a fun weekend event; or to celebrate an occasion like a shower in a relaxed, comfortable way. It's less pressured than an evening cocktail party or dinner, and most of these recipes can be made ahead of time. Don't hesitate to purchase some things ready-made—such as the coffee cake, Bundt cakes, or dessert—to lighten the load.

menu

ASPARAGUS SALAD WITH
PROSCIUTTO

CARROT GINGER SOUP

CHEESE STRATA

MIXED BERRY
AND YOGURT CARAMEL

MINI PUMPKIN BUNDT CAKES

APPLE COFFEECAKE

FRESH JUICES AND COFFEE

the setting

This menu is designed to be made ahead of time and can be served at room temperature, which frees up your serving options—you could even serve it outdoors. Set up foods as a buffet on a sideboard, island, or table, so guests can help themselves and then settle in somewhere comfy, like the living room. Plop big pillows on the floor for impromptu seating and lounging, and keep the mood relaxed with simple wildflower bouquets in glass jars. If you're hosting sleepover guests, the aromas of food will lure them downstairs, where you can encourage everyone to stay cozy in robes and pj's.

Flatware is easily—and prettily—managed by being tucked with the napkin inside a napkin ring for portability. Stand napkin in a napkin ring; add in silverware. Plain white napkin rings are dressed up with paper scrapbook embellishments.

Mix fresh juice blends like orange carrot, grapefruit tangerine and pineapple coconut (fresh-squeeze if desired) the night before and place in the refrigerator to chill. Serve on the buffet in individual glass milk bottles nestled inside ice-filled glasses to keep juices chilled and to make it easy for people to serve themselves.

Apple coffee cake is best made the day before so the flavors can meld. Fresh apple slices make the cake moist and flavorful. Spread small stations of food and flowers around the room so there's always a delicious treat within reach. Using just one type of flower simplifies arranging—pick flowers from your backyard, or buy at a local market the day before. Use a glass decanter for the buffet arrangement and the milk bottles for smaller satellite arrangements around the room.

Dress up a simple pound cake from the bakery with an easy lemon glaze and poppy seeds.

Glaze:
2/3 cup sifted confectioners' sugar
2 tablespoons lemon juice, fresh
1 teaspoon grated lemon rind
3 tablespoons poppy seeds

1. Put the sugar in a small bowl. Add lemon juice and rind. Whisk together until smooth and well blended.
2. Drizzle over pound cake and sprinkle with poppy seeds.

Silverware and napkins are tucked into napkin rings for easy access on a buffet. Fold cloth napkin in quarters, then in half vertically, then fold each side in, creating a trifold. Tuck bottom into napkin ring; add silverware. Ice-filled glass tumblers serve as mini ice buckets for individual juice bottles. A cake stand creates extra space on a buffet by going vertical. Small appetizer bowls offer just-right portion sizes for the soup and can balance on a plate with food. The large glass cylinder makes an ideal tureen to show off the beautiful color of the ginger carrot soup.

Eggcups make charming individual creamers for coffee and tea served in the handleless mugs on hors d'oeuvres plates. Make dishes in individual portions—like the mini bundt cakes—for easy serving. Place the cakes into a large mixing bowl for a simple, compact, and unexpected presentation.

the recipes

asparagus salad with prosciutto

Asparagus adds distinctive flavor to this salad, where it's paired with fresh herbs, tomatoes, and grated hard-boiled eggs.

SAVORY VINAIGRETTE

⅓   cup olive oil
2   tablespoons white wine vinegar
½   teaspoon Dijon mustard
1   clove garlic, minced
¼   teaspoon salt
¼   teaspoon freshly ground black pepper

ASPARAGUS SALAD

24   fresh asparagus spears
12   thin slices prosciutto, cut in half crosswise (about 8 ounces)
24   thin slices red bell pepper (about 1 pepper)
8   cups torn mixed salad greens such as radicchio, spinach, arugula, and chicory (12 to 16 ounces)
1   tablespoon minced fresh basil
½   cup red or yellow grape or cherry tomatoes (or a mixture), cut in half
2   large hard-boiled eggs, grated

1. Prepare the vinaigrette: In a blender, combine all of the vinaigrette ingredients. Cover and process until combined. Set aside.

2. Prepare the salad: Snap off and discard the woody base from the asparagus spears. If desired, scrape the scales from the stalks. Place the asparagus in a skillet with just enough lightly salted water to cover. Cover the skillet, bring to a rapid boil over high heat, and cook until the asparagus is crisp-tender, 3 to 5 minutes. Drain well, rinse with cold water, and drain again.

3. Using a pastry brush, brush an asparagus spear with some of the vinaigrette. Wrap a piece of prosciutto around the spear and a red bell pepper slice, leaving the tip of the asparagus showing; place the bundle on a plate. Repeat with the remaining prosciutto, asparagus, and red pepper slices.

4. In a large bowl, toss the greens with half the remaining vinaigrette and the basil. Arrange the greens on a large serving platter and top with the asparagus bundles. Arrange the tomatoes over the salad. Sprinkle with the grated egg. Serve the salad with the remaining vinaigrette on the side.

Serves 8 (makes about ½ cup Savory Vinaigrette)

Simplify: Use a favorite ready-made salad dressing to reduce your prep time.

carrot ginger soup

This delicious soup is equally tasty hot or at room temperature, so it is a perfect addition in any season.

- 6 tablespoons (⅓ stick) unsalted butter
- 1 large yellow onion, chopped
- ¼ cup finely chopped peeled fresh gingerroot
- 3 cloves garlic, minced
- 7 cups chicken stock
- 1 cup dry white wine
- 1½ pounds carrots, peeled and cut into ½-inch pieces
- 2 tablespoons fresh lemon juice
  Pinch curry powder
  Salt and freshly ground black pepper
- 3 tablespoons cream
  Snipped fresh chives or parsley for garnish

1. In a large stockpot, melt the butter over medium heat. Add the onion, ginger, and garlic and cook, stirring frequently, for 15 to 20 minutes. Add the stock, wine, and carrots. Bring the mixture to boiling over high heat. Reduce the heat to medium and simmer the mixture, uncovered, until the carrots are very tender, about 45 minutes.

2. Purée the soup in the pot with a handheld immersion blender (or in batches in a food processor) until smooth and creamy. Season with the lemon juice and curry powder; add salt and pepper to taste. Swirl cream on top as a garnish. Sprinkle with chives or parsley. Serve hot or at room temperature.

Serves 8

Simplify: Purchase frozen chopped carrots—you won't need to peel or slice them.

cheese strata

Be sure to assemble this breakfast casserole the night before so the bread has time to absorb the egg mixture. For a special treat, you can use artisanal bread from a favorite baker and real Parmigiano-Reggiano cheese for delicious results.

3   **tablespoons unsalted butter**

1   **medium onion, thinly sliced (1 cup)**

4   **scallions, white and green parts, finely chopped**

10   **slices ¼-inch thick, hearty white bread, lightly toasted and cut in half crosswise**

8   **slices cooked bacon, chopped into ½-inch pieces**

6   **ounces Parmesan cheese, finely grated (1 cup)**

8   **ounces Gruyère cheese, coarsely grated (2 cups)**

10   **large eggs**

2   **cups milk**

2   **teaspoons kosher or sea salt**

1   **teaspoon freshly ground black pepper**

1. In a medium sauté pan over medium-high heat, melt 1 tablespoon of the butter. Add the onion and cook, stirring, until translucent, 3 to 4 minutes. Add the scallions and cook, stirring, until they turn bright green, about 2 minutes more. Remove the pan from the heat and let the contents cool to room temperature.

2. Grease the bottom of a large baking dish with the remaining 2 tablespoons butter. Line the bottom of the dish with half the pieces of bread (slices can overlap). Sprinkle an even layer of bacon on top of the bread. Spoon on the onion and scallion mixture and sprinkle with both cheeses. Arrange the remaining bread slices in overlapping rows on top.

3. In a medium bowl, whisk together the eggs and milk until well combined. Whisk in the salt and pepper. Pour the egg mixture over the bread in the baking dish. Gently push the bread into the egg mixture. Cover the dish with foil and refrigerate for 8 to 10 hours or overnight.

4. Preheat the oven to 375°F.

5. Bake the foil-covered strata for 20 minutes, then remove the foil and bake for 20 minutes longer until the top is golden brown.

Serves 10

Simplify: Chop up some sliced deli ham instead of cooking bacon.

mixed berry and yogurt caramel

A sweet caramel topping adds a surprise to fresh berries and yogurt—this is so easy, you can whip it together at the very last minute.

4	cups plain yogurt
½	pint raspberries
½	pint blueberries
½	pint strawberries, hulled and cut in half
½	cup bottled caramel sauce

In a 9 x 13-inch baking dish or serving bowl, spoon the yogurt over the bottom. Scatter the berries over the yogurt. Heat the caramel on low in the microwave for 40 seconds. Pour the sauce over the yogurt and fruit and serve immediately.

Serves 8

Simplify: Arrange the ingredients in individual serving bowls before pouring the sauce—one less dish to wash!

mini pumpkin bundt cakes

Pumpkin purée gives these fluted muffins moistness and a fresh autumn flavor.

1½ **cups all-purpose flour**
½ **teaspoon salt**
1 **cup sugar**
1 **teaspoon baking soda**
1 **cup pumpkin purée**
½ **cup olive oil**
2 **large eggs, beaten**
¼ **cup water**
¼ **teaspoon ground nutmeg**
¼ **teaspoon ground cinnamon**
¼ **teaspoon ground allspice**

BROWN SUGAR GLAZE

½ **cup packed light brown sugar**
½ **teaspoon vanilla extract**
2 **tablespoons water**
½ **cup raw pumpkin seeds, for garnish**

1. Preheat the oven to 350°F. Generously butter 6 mini Bundt pans.

2. In a large bowl, sift together the flour, salt, sugar, and baking soda. In a medium bowl, stir together the pumpkin, oil, eggs, water, and all the spices. Add the pumpkin mixture to the flour mixture, stirring with a wooden spoon until just combined.

3. Pour the batter into the prepared pans. Bake for 40 to 45 minutes, until the tops are brown and a skewer inserted near the center of one comes out clean. Turn out the cakes onto wire racks to cool for 10 minutes.

4. Prepare the glaze: Combine all the glaze ingredients in a medium bowl, mixing with a wooden spoon until a liquid glaze forms. Using a pastry brush, brush the glaze over the tops of the cooled cakes and sprinkle with pumpkin seeds.

Makes 6 individual mini Bundt cakes

Simplify: Purchase ready-made pumpkin muffins and top them with the Brown Sugar Glaze and some sunflower seeds.

Place the mini Bundt cakes into one large mixing bowl for a simple, compact presentation.

apple coffeecake

Sections of fresh apple make this buttery cake especially moist. It can be made a day in advance.

½ **cup (1 stick) unsalted butter, plus 2 teaspoons for greasing pan**
1½ **cups packed light brown sugar**
2 **large eggs**
2 **cups all-purpose flour**
1 **teaspoon baking soda**
1 **teaspoon ground cinnamon**
½ **teaspoon salt**
1 **cup sour cream**
1 **teaspoon vanilla extract**
2 **cups peeled, sliced apples**

CRUMBLE TOPPING

½ **cup packed light brown sugar**
½ **cup all-purpose flour**
½ **teaspoon ground cinnamon**
4 **tablespoons unsalted butter, softened**

1. Preheat the oven to 350°F. Grease a 9-inch glass baking dish with the 2 teaspoons of butter.

2. In a large bowl, using an electric mixer on medium speed, beat the remaining ½ cup of butter and the brown sugar until light and fluffy. Keeping the mixer on medium speed, add the eggs one at a time, beating well after each addition.

3. In a separate bowl, sift together the flour, baking soda, cinnamon, and salt. With the mixer on low speed, add the flour mixture to the butter mixture in three parts, alternating with the sour cream. Beat until just combined after each addition. Beat in the vanilla. Using a rubber spatula, fold in the apples. Pour the batter into the prepared baking dish, spreading out to the edges.

4. Prepare the topping: In a small bowl, combine all the topping ingredients, stirring with a wooden spoon until the mixture resembles coarse crumbs. Sprinkle the topping evenly over the batter.

5. Bake the cake until the topping is golden brown and the cake is set, 35 to 40 minutes. Transfer the cake to a wire rack and cool in the pan for at least 10 minutes.

Serves 8

Simplify: Start with a packaged mix for crumb-topped coffeecake and add apple slices to the batter.

shhh! don't tell them it's takeout

When friends from out of town call up unexpectedly, or you want to have a spur-of-the-moment get-together, don't panic. With the great take-out restaurants and gourmet food shops these days, it is perfectly acceptable to let someone else do the cooking. What isn't so inviting is serving people out of cardboard take-out containers. Here, ways to dress up traditional Chinese takeout to make it a feast.

menu

SKEWERED SHRIMP

SAUTÉED STRING BEANS

COLD SESAME NOODLES

VEGETABLE ROLLS

BEEF AND VEGETABLE SAUTÉ

GREEN TEA ICE CREAM
WITH CHOCOLATE-DIPPED
FORTUNE COOKIES

the setting

Just because it's take-out doesn't mean it isn't worthy of the dining room, but you could also serve this meal at a kitchen island, coffee table, or as an outdoor picnic. Rich greens create a clean, festive feel for an Asian meal; add punch with vivid napkins and flatware holders, lush chartreuse orchids, and shimmering vellum-sheathed votives.

Origami is the inspiration for a folded and stitched paper flatware holder. Cut a piece of brightly colored or patterned paper into a 3 x 11-inch rectangle. Fold up 4 inches from the bottom and crease. Stitch up each side and across bottom with a sewing machine. For words and graphic motifs shown here, download pattern at www.entertainingsimple.com.

eat: drink: celebrate

Just a stem or two of elegant, long-lasting orchids are all you will need for a centerpiece. Snip blossoms and float in the rectangular tray.

Tall, handmade paper parasols brighten drink glasses and the table. Cut from patterned scrapbook paper with scallop-edge scissors; wrap around a skewer and join edges with a glue stick. A glass tumbler becomes a votive holder sheathed in vellum that's been stamped with motifs in white ink for subtle tone-on-tone texture. Download templates for paper umbrellas and votive holder sleeve at www.entertainingsimple.com.

Serve it with style: Instead of paper takeout cartons, elevate vegetable rolls on a cake stand; serve up beef and broccoli in an oval baking dish; decant sauces into glass votive holders. Shrimp skewers become inviting finger food stashed in the small mixing bowl. A glass compote accented with tall paper umbrellas makes a fun "scorpion bowl" drink for friends to share. Take fortune cookies from mundane to decadent by dipping them in melted dark chocolate and sprinkling with silver dragées. Green tea ice cream, opposite, scooped into glass tumblers, makes a refreshing finale.

summer barbecue

Take advantage of the fresh, homegrown foods of the season from your garden or the local farmers' market to serve a meal bursting with bright, simple flavors. This menu is easy to make ahead and serve as an afternoon lunch, or as a festive dinner under the glow of tiki torches at night. Celebrate a summer event such as a graduation, Father's Day, or the Fourth of July with this easygoing weekend get-together.

menu

**HERB-GRILLED
BEEF TENDERLOIN**

CORN SALAD

GRILLED POTATOES ANNA

TOMATO BREAD SALAD

FRESH FRUIT SANGRIA

PEACH SHORTCAKE

Fresh-picked flowers from the garden, like these vibrant zinnias, are all it takes to brighten the table. Votive candles are placed inside small hors d'oeuvres bowls and ringed with cut dill blossoms (or choose any other fragrant herb, such as lavender, from your garden). Instead of one centerpiece, place individual stems in a series of glass bottles and tumblers down the center of the table.

the setting

With a summery night as the star, you don't have to do much to make the evening magical. Dress a simple table in a colorful swath of fabric that highlights the flowers from your garden, add plenty of candlelight for a warm glow, and fresh-picked herbs for fragrance.

A strand of buttons or beads from the crafts store makes a simple and cheerful napkin ring around a crisp white napkin. Tie or hot-glue the ends together.

Keep the mood relaxed and casual: Place a table with a mix of chairs (whether indoor or outdoor) on the patio or deck, or even out on the lawn, beneath the canopy of a tree. Call the party for just before twilight, so you can get food grilled and to the table before it's dark, but also enjoy the setting sun and cooling air. Don't hesitate to enlist guests to help tote food to the table—it makes people feel more at ease to be given a task!

The natural bounty of the garden and farm stand are all you need to set a beautiful table. For a super-easy arrangement, place individual zinnia stems in glass bottles and tumblers down the center of the table. Intersperse with fresh peaches perched on eggcup "pedestals." A coral tablecloth picks up on the fruit and flowers' hues; you can easily make your own by buying about 2 1/2 yards of fabric and using iron-on fusing tape to form a hem at each end. Votive candles ringed with dill blossoms cast a pretty glow; choose citronella votives to ward off bugs.

The peaches on the table are a nod to the gorgeous dessert—shortcake layered with whipped cream and fresh sliced peaches. A refreshing white-wine sangria sparkles with jewel-like fruit slices as well, including raspberries, peaches, and plums. Be sure to make up extra batches in advance, and keep a pitcher on the table so it's easy for guests to help themselves.

the recipes

herb-grilled beef tenderloin

This easy-to-make main course is a perfectly seasoned, sophisticated star of the summer barbecue.

6	tablespoons olive oil
8	large cloves garlic, minced
2	tablespoons minced fresh rosemary
1	tablespoon dried thyme
2	tablespoons coarsely ground black pepper
1	tablespoon salt
1	beef tenderloin (5 pounds), trimmed

1. In a small bowl, mix together the oil, garlic, rosemary, thyme, pepper, and salt. Rub the oil-herb mixture over the tenderloin, coating evenly. Set the meat aside while you heat the grill to very hot.

2. Place the meat on the rack in the grill and close the lid; cook until well-seared, about 5 minutes. Turn the meat and cook (with the lid closed) until well-seared on the second side, 5 minutes more.

3. Move the meat to the cool side of the grill (if charcoal) or turn off the burner directly underneath the meat and adjust the other burners to medium. Cook until an instant-read thermometer inserted in the thickest part of the meat registers 130°F (for medium rare), 45 to 60 minutes, depending on the tenderloin size and grill. Transfer the meat to a clean platter and let it rest for 15 minutes before carving.

Serves 8 to 10

corn salad

Take advantage of the best fresh corn of the season to make this crunchy salad.

8   medium ears fresh corn, husks and silk removed
3   scallions, green parts only, finely minced
2   tablespoons chopped fresh thyme
3   large hard-boiled eggs, chopped
1   red bell pepper, cut into ½-inch strips
1   orange bell pepper, cut into ½-inch strips
4   slices of cooked bacon, finely chopped
¼   cup mayonnaise
1   teaspoon salt
½   teaspoon freshly ground black pepper
1   pint grape tomatoes, cut in half if desired

1. Bring a large pot of salted water to boiling. Add the corn; cover and boil for 1 minute. Drain the corn and cool under cold running water. Hold each ear, pointed-end up, on a cutting board and use a sharp knife to slice the kernels off the cob. You should have about 4 cups of kernels.

2. In a large bowl, stir together the corn, scallions, thyme, eggs, red and orange peppers, and bacon. Stir in the mayonnaise, salt, and black pepper and toss well. Cover and refrigerate for several hours to develop the flavors. Mix in the tomatoes just before serving.

Serves 8

Simplify: Cook the corn and eggs ahead of time; refrigerate until ready to prepare the salad.

grilled potatoes anna

Grill the herb-seasoned potatoes in foil to add extra flavor to this perfect complement to grilled meats.

- **4   russet potatoes, peeled and thinly sliced**
- **2   tablespoons olive oil**
- **2   teaspoons fresh thyme leaves**
-     **Dash fresh lemon juice**
-     **Salt and freshly ground black pepper**

1. Heat the grill to medium. Oil 2 squares of aluminum foil.

2. Combine in a large bowl the potatoes, oil, lemon juice, thyme, and salt and pepper to taste; toss to mix. Arrange the potato slices in layers on one foil square; transfer to the rack in the grill and cook for 3 to 4 minutes. Place the remaining square of foil oiled side down on top of the potatoes and crimp the edges together. Flip the sandwich over very carefully, supporting it with large spatulas on top and bottom. Remove the top foil square; cook 3 to 4 minutes more or until the potatoes are browned and cooked through.

Serves 4

Simplify: If your grill is too crowded, layer the seasoned potatoes in an oiled baking dish; cover and bake at 450°F for 30 minutes. Uncover and cook a few minutes more, until the top layer begins to brown.

tomato bread salad

The bread absorbs all the delicious juice of the tomatoes, making this incredibly easy salad incredibly tasty, too.

6	slices day-old country-style bread, cut into 1-inch pieces
1½	pounds ripe tomatoes, cut into 1-inch chunks
1	small sweet onion, finely chopped
¼	cup shredded fresh basil
¼	cup balsamic vinegar
6	tablespoons olive oil
	Salt and freshly ground black pepper

In a large bowl, toss together the bread, tomatoes, onion, and basil. In a separate small bowl, whisk together the vinegar and oil and pour over the bread mixture. Toss the salad well; season with salt and pepper. Serve immediately.

Serves 6

Simplify: Use bottled salad dressing instead of the vinegar and oil.

fresh fruit sangria

A light, fresh, and fruity tropical drink. Make sure it's very cold before you serve it; adding ice will dilute the flavor.

- 1 **peach, pitted and thinly sliced**
- 1 **plum, pitted and thinly sliced**
- 1 **nectarine, pitted and thinly sliced**
- 1 **pint raspberries**
- 1 **liter dry white wine (such as sauvignon blanc), chilled**
- 1 **cup orange liqueur (such as Triple Sec), chilled**

Place all of the fruit in a large pitcher. Pour in the wine and liqueur. Cover the sangria and refrigerate until ready to serve. When serving, use a spoon to place a small amount of fruit into each glass.

Serves 6

Simplify: Use thawed frozen sliced fruit instead of fresh.

peach shortcake

This is a delicious and old-fashioned way to celebrate whichever fruit is in season. Try blueberries, raspberries, or plums instead of peaches for an equally tasty dessert.

⅓   cup cold unsalted butter, cut into pieces
3   cups all-purpose flour
1   tablespoon plus 1 teaspoon baking powder
1   teaspoon salt
1   teaspoon ground cinnamon
½   cup firmly packed light brown sugar
½   cup coarsely chopped pecans
⅓   cup milk
1   large egg
8 to 10 medium peaches (about 2 pounds)
1½   cups sugar
1   cup heavy cream
¼   teaspoon almond extract or ½ teaspoon vanilla extract

1. Preheat the oven to 450°F. Turn 2 nine-inch round cake pans upside down and grease the pan bottoms.

2. In a large bowl, sift the flour, baking powder, salt, and cinnamon. Stir in the brown sugar. Using a pastry blender or two knives, cut in the butter until the mixture is crumbly. Stir in the pecans.

3. In a small bowl, whisk together the milk and egg. Add the milk mixture to the flour mixture; stir with a fork until blended. Spread the pastry on the upturned pans, dividing equally and leaving a ½-inch margin around the edge. Bake the pastry for 20 minutes, or until golden. Transfer the shortcakes from the pans to wire racks to cool.

4. Meanwhile, peel the peaches and slice them into a medium bowl. Stir in the sugar, ½ cup at a time, tasting the peaches for sweetness. In a small bowl, whip the cream with the almond or vanilla extract until stiff. When ready to serve, place 1 shortcake on a plate, top with half the peaches and half the whipped cream. Place the second shortcake on top and add the remaining peaches and whipped cream.

Serves 8

Simplify: Purchase ready-made biscuits at a farm stand or bakery so you don't have to heat up the kitchen.

3

entertaining a crowd

Sometimes it's easier to hit lots of birds with one stone and get your entertaining obligations accomplished all at once, and other times a big group is the best way to celebrate an important

occasion. Just remember, when the guest list grows, your anxiety doesn't have to increase along with it. Cooking in greater quantity may take a little more time, but it shouldn't be more complex. In fact, the bigger the party, the simpler the food should be. This is also the time to hit the local caterer, prepared-food store, or bakery to taste test a few things you could buy ready-made. Then try to choose mostly recipes that can be made ahead, and also things that are easy to serve, so that you can show up to your own party calm, cool, and collected rather than frazzled, overheated, and overwhelmed.

girl talk

This is a modern take on the tea party, with flavorful iced and hot teas and a casual buffet of sweet and savory foods. Whether you're hosting a shower, your book group, the neighbor-hood moms, a birthday party or a mini reunion, this is the perfect light and easy menu to keep the conversation and laughter flowing. Almost everything can be prepared in advance. To make it even simpler, buy some of the elements already prepared.

menu

LOBSTER AND AVOCADO SALAD

CHEESE AND TOMATO
MINI QUICHES

PETITE SHRIMP SALAD
SANDWICHES

BERRY PLUM COMPOTE

SPICY GINGER CAKE

RASPBERRY TEA PUNCH

the setting

Adapt the Japanese teahouse tradition of sitting on the floor to create a young, inviting ambience that works well in an apartment or other small-space living arrangement. Place soft, colorful throw pillows and cushions around a coffee table to set the stage for a relaxed, unstuffy gathering. You can set the coffee table as you would a dining table, with plates, flatware, and colorful napkins displayed beneath glass salad plates. Printed cocktail napkins add a hit of a lively pattern. Informal groupings of single-stem peonies placed in glass mugs and bottles are lush and feminine, yet couldn't be simpler to arrange. You could also choose roses, daisies, lilies, or another flower from your garden. This party also works well outdoors, where again, blankets and pillows can help extend seating options.

serving ideas

Make ice cubes in long slender sticks (using a special ice tray, available at IKEA and other housewares stores) with pieces of lemon zest and lemon thyme frozen inside. Place the ice sticks in glass tumblers and serve with ice water or punch.

Tea sandwiches are served on a platter decorated with a scalloped piece of striped vellum paper, for an updated "doily." Cut a piece of paper ½ inch smaller than the interior of the platter. Using a ruler with a scalloped edge, trace the pattern and cut.

Serve the hot tea with cups of lemon drops for sweetening, instead of sugar.

Perch the cake on one of the throw pillows like a favored guest!

Serve the lobster salad in hors d'oeuvres bowls for perfect small portions that won't break the bank.

party countdown

This is a suggested countdown for the tea, but you can adapt it to any party.

Three or more days before:

☒ Plan your menu and decide what you will make and what, if anything, you will buy ready-made. Write a shopping list of all ingredients, foods, beverages, and any paper products you'll need.

☒ Decide on a color palette and order or shop for flowers to coordinate.

Two days before:

☒ Shop for all ingredients, beverages, and paper products.

Day before:

☒ Prepare and bake quiche (refrigerate).

☒ Bake ginger cake.

☒ Arrange platters.

☒ Pick up any prepared foods (except baked goods).

Day of party:

☒ Pick up flowers and any last-minute items or prepared foods.

☒ Make icing and decorate cake.

☒ Mix shrimp salad and make sandwiches.

☒ Make lobster salad and vinaigrette.

☒ Remove quiche from refrigerator and bring to room temperature (about 2 hours before serving).

☒ Make punch and chill. Add ice just before serving.

☒ Set table and place single stem flowers in bottles and cups.

the recipes

lobster and avocado salad

Each petite serving of this salad boasts enough lobster to be a decadent indulgence.

DRESSING

½   **cup olive oil**
2   **teaspoons kosher salt**
½   **teaspoon garlic powder**
¼   **cup ketchup**
1   **teaspoon Dijon mustard**

SALAD

3   **cups mixed salad greens (mesclun)**
1   **cup cooked lobster meat, broken into small pieces**
1   **avocado, peeled, pitted, and sliced into 12 pieces**
6   **thin lemon slices**
    Fresh oregano sprigs, for garnish

1. Prepare the dressing: In a small bowl combine all of the dressing ingredients. Mix thoroughly with a wire whisk.

2. Prepare the salad: In a medium bowl, combine the greens, lobster, avocado, and lemon slices. Add half the dressing and toss to coat.

3. Divide the salad among 6 small bowls and garnish with oregano sprigs. Serve the extra dressing on the side.

Serves 6

Simplify: Start with thawed frozen cooked lobster or shrimp to get ahead of the game.

Serve the lobster salad in hors
d'oeuvres bowls nestled inside
the rectangular baking dish.
Bring to the table with a cruet
of salad dressing.

cheese and tomato mini quiches

These cheese and tomato quiches can be made ahead of time and served at room temperature. I serve them right in the tart pans.

PASTRY

1¼	cups all-purpose flour
¼	teaspoon salt
¼	cup vegetable shortening
2	tablespoons cold unsalted butter
3 to 4 tablespoons cold water	

FILLING

2	tablespoons unsalted butter
1	tablespoon packed brown sugar
1	teaspoon apple cider vinegar
2	medium onions, quartered lengthwise and thinly sliced (about 1⅓ cups)
4	ounces feta cheese, crumbled (1 cup)
4	large eggs
½	teaspoon dried marjoram, crushed
¼	teaspoon freshly ground black pepper
⅓	cup milk, half-and-half or light cream
3	tablespoons dry white wine or chicken broth
1	cup halved grape tomatoes
2	tablespoons snipped fresh chives
4	ounces sharp Cheddar cheese, shredded (1 cup)

1. Prepare the pastry: In the bowl of a food processor, combine the flour and salt. Add the shortening and butter and process for about 10 seconds, or until the mixture starts to resemble coarse crumbs. With the processor running, add the cold water by teaspoonfuls through the feed tube until the pastry just holds together without being wet or sticky. If it is crumbly, add a bit more water. (Note: To mix the crust by hand, use a pastry blender or two knives to cut in the shortening and butter until the pieces are pea-size. Sprinkle 1 tablespoon cold water over part of the flour mixture; gently toss with a fork. Push moistened flour to the side of the bowl. Repeat 3 to 4 times, until all of the flour mixture is moistened.) Form the pastry into a ball. Cover with plastic wrap and refrigerate for ½ hour.

2. Preheat the oven to 450°F.

3. Divide the pastry into 8 pieces. On a lightly floured surface roll each portion into a 5½-to 6-inch diameter round. Place each round in a 4-inch tart pan with a removable bottom. Using your fingers, press the dough onto the bottom and up the sides of each tart pan; trim the dough even with the rim of the pan.

4. Line the dough in each tart pan with heavy foil or a double thickness of regular foil. Place the pans on a large baking sheet and bake for 8 minutes. Remove the baking sheet from the oven; remove the foil from the tart shells. Return the sheet to the oven and continue baking the shells for 8 to 10 minutes more, or until the pastry is lightly browned. Transfer the shells on the baking sheet to a wire rack to cool. Decrease the oven temperature to 375°F.

5. Prepare the filling: Melt the butter in a medium skillet over medium heat; stir in the brown sugar and vinegar. Add the onions. Cook uncovered over medium-low heat, stirring occasionally, until the onions are tender and lightly browned, 12 to 15 minutes.

6. In a medium bowl, beat the feta cheese, eggs, marjoram, and pepper with an electric mixer on low speed until well combined. Stir in the onion mixture, milk, and wine.

7. Place four or five pieces of grape tomato in each tart shell on the baking sheet. Ladle the filling equally into the shells. Sprinkle with the chives and top with the Cheddar cheese.

8. Return the baking sheet with the filled pastry to the oven. Bake for 25 to 30 minutes or until a skewer inserted near the center of a tart comes out clean and the edges are golden. Transfer the tarts to a wire rack; cool for 15 minutes. Carefully remove the pan sides. Serve warm.

Serves 8

Simplify: Make this recipe up to two weeks in advance and freeze, individually wrapped, in the tart pans.

Use ready-made pie crust from the freezer instead of making the dough by hand.

Scalloped tart pans create a pretty and crisp crust. Serve the mini quiches right in their pans on a platter or cake stand.

petite shrimp salad sandwiches

Whole grain bread is the perfect complement to this savory shrimp salad. Use an artisanal loaf from your favorite baker.

1	pound large shrimp, peeled and cooked
¾	cup chopped celery
½	cup minced red onion
¼	cup chopped scallions, green parts only
2	tablespoons chopped green bell pepper
1¼	cups mayonnaise
1	tablespoon soy sauce
2	teaspoons yellow mustard
½	teaspoon garlic salt
2	tablespoons mixed snipped fresh lemon thyme, chives, and tarragon
1	loaf whole grain bread, sliced

1. In a medium bowl, combine the shrimp, celery, onion, scallions, and green pepper. In a small bowl, stir together 1 cup of the mayonnaise, the soy sauce, mustard, and garlic salt. Stir the mayonnaise mixture into the shrimp mixture. Stir in the thyme, chives, and tarragon. Cover and refrigerate for several hours.

2. Cut the bread slices into 3-inch squares. Spread the remaining ¼ cup mayonnaise over each of the squares. Top each square with a generous dollop of shrimp salad. Arrange the sandwiches on a platter; cover and refrigerate if not serving immediately.

Serves 6 to 8

Simplify: Start with ready-made shrimp salad from a good deli; all you'll have to do is follow step 2 to assemble sandwiches.

For an alternative, layer slivers of packaged smoked salmon atop the prepared bread for an easy, tasty substitute.

berry plum compote

These fresh fruit flavors are a great first course at any party. Add vanilla whipped cream, if desired, for an indulgent twist.

VANILLA WHIPPED CREAM

1	vanilla bean, sliced in half lengthwise
½	pint heavy cream
4	teaspoons sugar

FRUIT COMPOTE

½	pint strawberries, hulled and sliced
1	plum, pitted and sliced
½	pint blueberries
12	fresh mint leaves, for garnish

1. Prepare the whipped cream: Two hours prior to whipping, place one vanilla bean half in the container of cream; refrigerate while it steeps. Tightly wrap the remaining bean half and refrigerate for another use.

2. Pour the cream into a medium bowl; discard the bean. Add the sugar to the cream and beat until firm peaks form. The whipped cream may be refrigerated, covered, for up to 4 hours.

3. Prepare the compote: In a medium bowl, combine all of the fruit, stirring gently to mix. To serve, spoon the compote into 6 individual bowls; dollop with the whipped cream, and garnish each serving with 2 mint leaves.

Serves 6 (makes about 2 cups whipped cream)

Simplify: Purchase precut fruits, and add ready-made vanilla-flavored whipped cream.

Fill a glass compote with
the fresh fruit salad
and add sprigs of mint to
enhance the flavors.

spicy ginger cake

This delicious cake is stunning with its glossy surface studded with sparkly barley candy—it always draws a crowd to the table. If white isn't what you have in mind, you can color the glaze with food coloring.

GINGER CAKE

2	cups molasses
1	cup sugar
2	cups vegetable oil
5	cups all-purpose flour
4	teaspoons ground cinnamon
2	teaspoons ground nutmeg
1	teaspoon cayenne pepper
2	cups water
4	teaspoons baking soda
4	large eggs, room temperature
½	pound fresh gingerroot, peeled, finely chopped

WHITE GLAZE

3	cups confectioners' sugar
¼	cup plus 2 teaspoons water
1	cup crushed pink and yellow barley candy

1. Preheat the oven to 350ºF. Grease two 9-inch round cake pans with shortening and line with parchment paper.

2. Prepare the cake: In a large bowl, stir together the molasses, sugar, and oil. In a medium bowl, sift together the flour, cinnamon, nutmeg, and cayenne pepper. In a small saucepan over high heat, bring the water to boil. Stir in the baking soda until it dissolves and then pour the hot water mixture into the molasses. Gradually whisk in the flour mixture. Whisk in the eggs, one at a time, and then the gingerroot. Continue whisking until the batter is glossy and well combined.

3. Pour the batter into the prepared pans. Bake for 1 hour, until the tops of the cakes spring back when lightly touched or a wooden toothpick inserted in a cake center comes out clean. If the tops of the cakes brown too quickly, cover with a piece of foil and continue baking. Transfer the cakes to a wire rack and cool in the pans for at least 30 minutes.

4. Prepare the glaze: In a large bowl, sift the confectioners' sugar. With a fork, stir in the water. The glaze should be spreadable. If it is too thin, add more confectioners' sugar, 1 tablespoon at a time. If it is too thick, add more water, 1 teaspoon at a time.

5. Run a spatula between the cake and pan sides to loosen the cakes; then turn out onto wire racks. Transfer one cake to a serving plate. Spoon the glaze over the cake and spread with an offset spatula. Place the other cake on top and cover the top and sides with glaze. Immediately top with the crushed barley candy.

Serves 10 (makes 2 cups glaze)

Simplify: Purchase ready-made gingerbread from a bakery or grocery store and top with the white glaze. If you can't find barley candy (an old-fashioned sugar candy) use crushed lollipops or other hard candy.

raspberry tea punch

Flavored by naturally sweet orange juice and fresh raspberry purée, this fruity tea punch requires no additional sugar.

2	cups orange juice
2	cups ruby red grapefruit juice
2	cups brewed Celestial Seasonings Red Zinger tea, or other herbal hibiscus-flavored tea
1	cup lemon-flavored seltzer water
1	cup puréed fresh raspberries
5	cups ice cubes
1	tablespoon fresh lemon thyme leaves
½	cup fresh whole raspberries

In a large bowl, combine the orange juice, grapefruit juice, tea, seltzer, and raspberry purée; mix thoroughly with a wire whisk. Stir in the ice cubes and thyme leaves. Top with fresh raspberries. Serve immediately.

Makes 16 four-ounce servings

Simplify: Combine 2 quarts prepared raspberry tea with 1 liter lemon-flavored seltzer and 5 cups ice cubes. Top with ½ cup fresh raspberries.

You don't need to buy a punch bowl: Show off the raspberry tea punch with fresh fruit in a large ceramic mixing bowl instead. Place on a dinner plate to catch the drips from condensation.

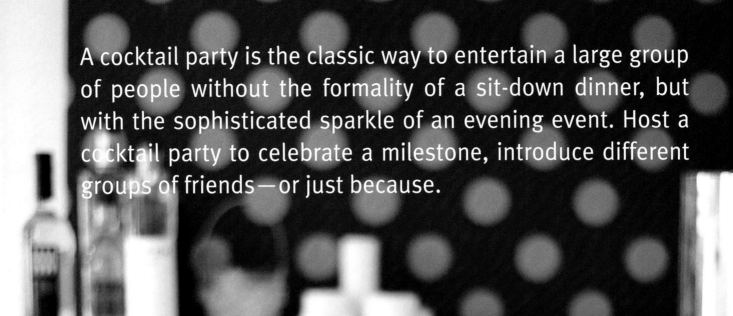

A cocktail party is the classic way to entertain a large group of people without the formality of a sit-down dinner, but with the sophisticated sparkle of an evening event. Host a cocktail party to celebrate a milestone, introduce different groups of friends—or just because.

good spirits cocktail party

menu

SHRIMP WITH FRESH TOMATO SALSA

PROSCIUTTO-WRAPPED GREEN BEAN BUNDLES

MARINATED OLIVES

HERBED GOAT CHEESE BITES

BRIOCHE ROUNDS WITH GOAT CHEESE, HONEY, AND FIGS

RED POTATOES WITH TOMATO-AVOCADO SALSA

GARLIC SHRIMP AND PESTO TOASTS

CHOCOLATE-TOPPED MINI VANILLA ICE CREAM CONES

PEAR GINGER BRANDY POPSICLES

SPIKED LEMONADE

the setting

A cocktail party is likely to center on the living room, but depending on the layout of your home, it is bound to spill over into other rooms. To help prevent the typical bottleneck in the kitchen, set up the bar elsewhere, and either pass hors d'oeuvres or have several small stations set up throughout the party space. A cocktail party is also ideal to host outdoors on a terrace, large porch, or lawn (add some tables and chairs so guests can rest their feet). Bowls of nibble foods, such as the olives and cheese bites, can be placed all over—on side and coffee tables, and at the bar. It's always nice to pass at least some hors d'oeuvres, especially the hot ones, so food doesn't grow cold sitting on a table and guests can help themselves to a bite without having to leave a conversation. An extravagant gesture, like the seafood tower, will create a focal point to draw guests to a buffet. Even at a cocktail party, it's fun to segue into more dessertlike treats later in the party.

Add luminous, romantic lighting by placing chunky pillar candles in various heights on a square plate. Music can help set the right vibe, especially at the beginning, as guests are just arriving, and the din of conversation hasn't yet filled the room. If you don't have a good collection of your own, borrow a music-savvy friend's iPod or go online and download some party mixes—iTunes has great playlists for every kind of music and mood.

serving ideas

A rolling cart or portable bar can be a boon at a cocktail party so you can set up an extra bar or hors d'oeuvres station in the living room or wherever desired. Smaller appetizer-size plates, bowls, and utensils help guests manage an hors d'oeuvre and drink more easily.

Create a dramatic seafood tower using simple nesting mixing bowls and a platter. Fill each of three bowls in graduated sizes with crushed ice. Make a well in the middle of the ice in the largest bowl, and place the medium bowl atop it. Do the same with that bowl and top it with the small bowl. Fill the three layers of the tower with 2 pounds each of steamed and chilled shrimp and mussels; 2 medium steamed lobster pieces in the shell; and 3 to 4 sliced lemons. Top off with a lobster tail.

Set up glasses in advance of the party with fresh fruit twists and stirrers. Give swizzle sticks extra sparkle with vintage rhinestone jewels (and help guests keep track of their drinks). Buy inexpensive orphan earrings, brooches, or shoe clips at tag sales or flea markets. Remove the backs using wire cutters. Affix the jewels to a metal cocktail stirrer with sparing amounts of hot glue.

Glass votive holders are particularly versatile helpers at a cocktail party. They can be used to hold sauces, small appetizers, lemon wedges, and other bar accoutrements, toothpicks, even olive pits. And of course, candles. Glass tumblers can hold small appetizers like olives, nuts, or goat-cheese bites. Place on tables around the room.

Pecans, top right, are spiced with Herbes de Provence and roasted in the oven at 400°F for 20 to 30 minutes. Garnish with sprigs of rosemary. Goat cheese bites rolled in herbs, near right (see recipe on page 124), can be stacked in a glass tumbler and served with a drizzle of olive oil and fresh peppercorns.

Icy limoncello (an Italian lemon-flavored liqueur) is served in chilled votive holders, left, with wedges of fresh lemon. Irresistible popsicles for grown-ups, right, feature ginger, brandy, and pear puree. (See page 130 for recipe.) Serve in eggcups for a nifty way to contain drips.

the recipes

shrimp with fresh tomato salsa

When you serve this spicy fresh salsa with shrimp, you'll banish cocktail sauce forever.

6	plum tomatoes, seeded and diced
½	cup diced yellow onion
1	jalapeño chile, seeded and diced (see note)
2	cloves garlic, minced
2	tablespoons minced fresh parsley
1	tablespoon minced fresh cilantro
1	teaspoon crushed dried oregano
2	tablespoons olive oil
1	tablespoon red wine vinegar
¼	teaspoon salt
⅛	teaspoon freshly ground black pepper
2	dozen cooked shrimp

In a medium bowl, mix together all of the ingredients except for the shrimp; toss well. Cover and refrigerate for 8 to 10 hours to allow the flavors to blend and fully develop. Serve with the shrimp.

Makes 3½ cups

Note: Wear rubber gloves when seeding the chile.

Simplify: Purchase a good-quality ready-made salsa at a grocery store or Mexican take-out restaurant.

An individual serving of shrimp fits neatly in a glass votive holder, nestled in tomato salsa with a sprig of fresh oregano. Pair it with a small hors d'oeuvres plate and cocktail napkin.

prosciutto-wrapped green bean bundles

These crisp bites of green bean are fresh and made delicious by the salty Italian ham.

1	pound fresh green beans, trimmed
¼	cup olive oil
	Salt and freshly ground black pepper
12	slices prosciutto, cut in half lengthwise
	Herb-infused olive oil, for drizzling

1. Bring a medium pot of water to boiling. Add the beans and boil until they are just tender and turn bright green, about 3 minutes. Drain the beans and plunge in ice water to stop the cooking; drain well. Toss them in the olive oil and season with salt and pepper to taste.

2. Bundle the beans in groups of 5 and wrap 1 piece of prosciutto around each bundle. Arrange the bundles on a serving platter and drizzle with the herb-infused oil.

Serves 12

Simplify: Start with steamed green beans from a salad bar or Chinese take-out restaurant.

marinated olives

Seasoned olives are the perfect complement to mixed drinks—put a tumbler full by the bar.

1	pound large green olives, drained
1	pound Kalamata olives, drained
1	sprig fresh rosemary
1	sprig fresh thyme
2	tablespoons chopped fresh oregano leaves
2	bay leaves
3	large cloves garlic, smashed
2	tablespoons whole black peppercorns
1	teaspoon red pepper flakes
1	cup olive oil, or as needed
⅓	cup white wine vinegar, or as needed

In a large glass bowl, combine both types of olives, the rosemary, thyme, oregano, bay leaves, garlic, black peppercorns, and hot pepper flakes; toss to mix. Transfer the mixture to a glass jar or plastic container with a tight lid. Add enough oil and vinegar to cover the olives halfway, using 3 parts oil to 1 part vinegar. Marinate overnight for the best flavor. Store in the refrigerator for up to 3 months. To serve, use a slotted spoon to transfer the olives to a bowl; return the rosemary, thyme sprigs, and bay leaves to the container with the unused olives.

Makes 4 cups

Simplify: Buy marinated olives from the deli or gourmet grocery and add snips of fresh herbs when serving.

herbed goat cheese bites

These morsels of savory goat cheese can be enjoyed with crackers, peasant breads, and marinated olives. Use a very good extra virgin olive oil for maximum flavor and a mixture of red, green, white, and black peppercorns for color.

10	ounces soft goat cheese (such as Montrachet), softened
2	tablespoons fresh thyme leaves, minced
2	tablespoons snipped chives
1	tablespoon paprika
	Extra virgin olive oil, for drizzling
2	tablespoons crushed mixed peppercorns

1. Line a baking sheet with waxed paper. Pinch a small ¾ inch piece from the cheese and roll into a ball between your palms; place on the prepared baking sheet. Repeat until all the cheese is used (you should have about 16 balls). Cover with plastic wrap and refrigerate for at least 20 minutes.

2. Meanwhile, place the thyme, chives, and paprika into individual small bowls (or arrange in separate piles on waxed paper). Divide the cheese balls into four groups, one for each bowl of seasoning. Roll the balls, one at a time, in one seasoning each, pressing slightly so that the cheese is covered; return the balls to the baking sheet as you go and refrigerate for one hour until set.

3. Place the cheese balls in a glass tumbler. Drizzle with olive oil and sprinkle with the crushed peppercorns.

Makes about 16 bite-size balls

Simplify: Purchase goat cheese that has already been rolled in seasonings, such as cracked pepper or lavender and thyme from the gourmet cheese section of your grocery store.

brioche rounds with goat cheese, honey, and figs

These fresh ingredients mixed together create a crunchy, salty-sweet taste experience.

1	loaf brioche, cut into twelve ½-inch thick slices
8	ounces soft goat cheese (such as Montrachet)
6	slices prosciutto, cut in half crosswise
6	fresh ripe figs, cut in half
	Honey, for drizzling
	Fresh oregano leaves, for garnish

1. Preheat the oven to 300°F. Line a baking sheet with parchment paper.

2. Using a 3-inch diameter biscuit cutter, cut a round from each bread slice. Place the bread rounds on the prepared baking sheet and toast in the oven for 2 to 3 minutes, turning once. Transfer the bread rounds to wire racks to cool.

3. Spread some goat cheese on each bread round; top with a piece of prosciutto and a fig half. Drizzle honey on the rounds; garnish with fresh oregano.

Makes 12 rounds

Simplify: Start with ready-made bread crisps and skip turning on the oven.

red potatoes with tomato-avocado salsa

Starchy potato and fresh salsa make every bite a delightful mélange of flavors and textures.

12	medium red potatoes (4 pounds), scrubbed
½	cup olive oil
1	tablespoon kosher salt
1	tablespoon minced fresh rosemary leaves

TOMATO-AVOCADO SALSA

8 to 10	medium plum tomatoes, seeded and finely chopped (3 cups)
1	cup chopped scallions, green parts only
3	cloves garlic, minced
¼	cup olive oil
1	tablespoon fresh lemon juice
2	medium avocados, peeled, pitted, and coarsely chopped (2 cups)
½	teaspoon salt
¼	teaspoon freshly ground black pepper
	Full-fat sour cream, for garnish (optional)

1. Preheat the oven to 400°F. Lightly oil a large roasting pan.

2. Cut the potatoes into halves and place in a large bowl. Add the oil, salt, and rosemary, and toss until the potatoes are well coated. Arrange the potatoes, cut side down, in the prepared pan. Bake for 30 to 40 minutes until the potatoes are crisp and browned, stirring occasionally to keep the potatoes from sticking.

3. Prepare the salsa: In a large bowl, combine the tomatoes, onions, garlic, oil, and lemon juice. Gently mix in the avocados, salt, and pepper; adjust the seasoning if you wish. Arrange the warm potato quarters on large serving platter. Top with the salsa and, if desired, dollops of sour cream.

Serves 12

Simplify: Use a good ready-made salsa and guacamole for the topping.

garlic shrimp and pesto toasts

Using ready-made pesto for these quick and savory appetizers makes them a cinch.

12	slices cocktail rye bread
1	tablespoon unsalted butter
1	clove garlic, minced
12	medium shrimp, peeled and deveined (with tails intact if desired)
	Salt and freshly ground black pepper
¼	cup prepared basil pesto, sun-dried tomato pesto, or black olive spread
6	grape tomatoes, cut in half
3	tablespoons finely grated Parmesan cheese

1. Preheat the broiler.

2. Place the pumpernickel slices on a baking sheet. Broil the bread 4 to 5 inches from the heat for about 2 minutes per side or just until crisp. Remove the bread but keep the broiler heated.

3. In a medium skillet melt the butter over medium heat. Add the garlic and cook, stirring, for 1 minute. Add the shrimp and cook, stirring, until the shrimp are opaque, 3 to 4 minutes more. Season with salt and pepper.

4. Spread the pesto over the toasted bread slices. Top each slice with a shrimp and a tomato half; sprinkle with Parmesan cheese. Broil for 1 to 2 minutes or just until the cheese starts to melt.

Serves 12 as an appetizer

Simplify: Use cooked shrimp from the seafood or frozen food section of your market.

chocolate-topped mini vanilla ice cream cones

A swirl of rich chocolate ganache puts these little treats miles ahead of the classic ice cream cone. To make them even better, use an ice cream with bits of vanilla bean mixed throughout—each piece of bean is a burst of real vanilla flavor.

12	sugar cones
1	pint vanilla ice cream
	Chocolate Ganache (page 142)
	Sprinkles and silver dragées, for topping

1. Make the cones smaller by breaking off the top section of each cone with your fingers. With a pair of kitchen scissors, cut around the broken edge to make it smooth.

2. Fit a pastry bag with a number 12 star tip; add the ganache to the bag and set it aside. Spoon the ice cream into the cones, filling each to the top. Pipe a tight spiral of chocolate ganache on the top center of the ice cream. Sprinkle with the assorted dragées and sprinkles. Place in the freezer until ready to serve.

Serves 12

Simplify: Use premade mini cake cones; drizzle the ice cream with bottled chocolate sauce instead of making the ganache.

pear ginger brandy popsicles

2	tablespoons lemon juice concentrate
½	cup water
½	cup sugar
½	cup brandy
2	cups pear puree
1	teaspoon ground cinnamon
½	teaspoon ground ginger

In a small saucepan combine the lemon juice concentrate, water, sugar, and brandy. Bring to a boil over medium heat. Remove from the heat and let cool completely. Add the pear puree to the cooled syrup and mix until combined. Divide the mixture into two. Add cinnamon and ginger to one and stir until thoroughly mixed. In a freezer popsicle tray, add the mixtures in alternating layers, about a tablespoon per layer. Place the sticks in the tray and place in freezer until thoroughly frozen.

Mini ice cream cones get sophisticated shimmer from silver dragées and sprinkles atop a frosting of chocolate ganache. Anchor them in glass tumblers filled with more silver dragées to make serving easier—and prettier!

spiked lemonade

To make a nonalcoholic drink, substitute seltzer for the vodka.

¾	cup fresh lemon juice (4 lemons)
½	cup superfine sugar, more if preferred
2	cups water
	Ice cubes
1	pint raspberries
1	lemon, thinly sliced, for garnish
	Sprigs of fresh mint, for garnish
1½	cups vodka

In a large pitcher, stir together the lemon juice and sugar until the sugar dissolves. Add the water; stir and taste. Add more sugar if the mixture is too tart. Fill individual glasses with ice. Divide the raspberries among the glasses and add some lemon slices and a mint sprig to each glass. Stir the vodka into the lemonade. Pour the lemonade into the prepared glasses.

Serves 4 to 8 (makes 1 quart)

Simplify: Use ready-made lemonade and simply add the vodka and fruit.

coffeehouse

Warm up a winter afternoon or evening with this informal, help-yourself party. This is an inviting, cozy dessert party that is the perfect solution for after a concert or skating session, or a holiday party without the stress and prep work of serving

menu

**SUPER RICH CHOCOLATE
SANDWICH COOKIES**

COCONUT CAKE

PISTACHIO BISCUITS

BRAIDED COOKIES

BUTTER ALMOND STICKS

BROWN SUGAR SANDIES

**CHOCOLATE CUPCAKES WITH
PEANUT BUTTER FILLING**

TIRAMISU

MARSHMALLOW ESPRESSO

CHOCOLATE LATTE

the setting

Fire up the espresso machine (or brew different varieties of rich fresh-ground coffee), light the fire, and welcome guests to a warm and cozy coffeehouse filled with indulgent treats and interesting conversation. Choose a comfortable room with plenty of seating, whether it's the living room, family room, or kitchen/dining area. Flowers, candles, and napkins in neutral hues—cream, cocoa, and sand—echo the palette of the food and drinks. Decorations can be minimally elegant: Float flower blossoms (such as white roses, found easily even in winter) in a glass cylinder filled with water. With a wink and a nod to the menu, votive candles are nestled in a base of Demerara (raw) sugar inside glass tumblers, and tapers are anchored in glass milk bottles. Cocktail napkins and fabric sleeves for coffee mugs are made in café au lait colors as well.

Glass containers multitask in unexpected ways: A tower of chocolate sandwich cookies is stacked inside a celery vase; small votives are the perfect size for shots of espresso. Votive candles (in glass tumblers) and taper candles (in bottles) are anchored in raw sugar. Fragrant gardenia blossoms float in a glass cylinder for a couldn't-be-easier arrangement.

coffee holders

Make your own
reusable coffee
cup sleeves for
handleless mugs
out of fabric and
cardboard.

1. Cut two 5 x 12-inch rectangles of fabric. Cut both corners (about 2 inches) off one end to form a triangular point.

2. With right sides facing together, sew together using a ⅓-inch seam allowance. Leave the straight end open.

3. Turn right side out and iron. Sew around edges, using a ½-inch seam allowance. (The open end will not show when wrapped.)

4. Cut a piece of thin cardboard to fit inside. Slide inside the fabric sleeve.

5. Wrap fabric sleeve around handleless mug sideways. Hot-glue pointed end over open (unfinished) end. Finish by hot-gluing a button on the pointed end.

Simplify: Skip the sewing and use decorative socks by cutting off the heel and toe and slipping the calf section over the mug.

the recipes

super rich chocolate sandwich cookies

These are so scrumptious you'll want to make a double batch. You can prepare the Chocolate Ganache filling while the dough is chilling.

8	tablespoons (1 stick) cold unsalted butter, cut into pieces
½	cup confectioners' sugar
1	cup all-purpose flour
5	teaspoons cornstarch
2	tablespoons unsweetened cocoa powder
2	large eggs

CHOCOLATE GANACHE

7	(1-ounce) squares bittersweet chocolate
½	cup heavy cream
3	tablespoons unsalted butter
3	tablespoons brandy

1. Prepare the cookie dough: In a food processor, combine the butter, confectioners' sugar, flour, cornstarch, cocoa powder, and egg yolk; process until a soft dough forms. Wrap the dough in plastic wrap and refrigerate for 30 minutes.

2. Preheat the oven to 350°F. Line a baking sheet with parchment paper.

3. Roll tablespoonfuls of dough into balls; place on the prepared baking sheet and press with your fingers to slightly flatten. Bake for 5 to 7 minutes or until the bottoms of the cookies are lightly cooked. Transfer the cookies to wire racks; let cool.

4. Prepare the ganache: Place the chocolate, heavy cream, and butter in a small heavy saucepan. Cook over low heat, stirring frequently, until the chocolate is melted. Stir in the brandy. Remove from the heat. Allow the ganache to cool slightly so it thickens before using it as directed in the recipe.

5. To assemble the cookies, invert half of them, spread a small amount of ganache on each, and then place the remaining cookies on top.

Makes 12 filled cookies

Simplify: Begin with ready-made chocolate wafer cookies.

coconut cake

This simple layer cake has the sweet, moist quality of a freshly cut coconut.

½   **cup unsalted butter**
¾   **cup sugar**
1   **teaspoon vanilla extract**
2   **large eggs**
2   **cups all-purpose flour**
1   **tablespoon baking powder**
¼   **teaspoon salt**
½   **cup cream of coconut**
½   **cup whole milk**
1   **cup large pieces of shredded coconut, for topping**

COCONUT CUSTARD FILLING

2   **cups prepared vanilla pudding or custard**
½   **cup shredded coconut**
2   **drops coconut oil**

CREAM CHEESE ICING

4   **ounces cream cheese, softened**
¼   **cup butter, softened**
2   **teaspoons vanilla extract**
2½ to 3 **cups sifted confectioners' sugar**

1. Preheat the oven to 350°F. Grease the bottom of a 13 x 9 x 2-inch baking pan; set aside.

2. Prepare the cake: In a large mixing bowl, beat the ½ cup butter with an electric mixer on medium speed for 30 seconds. Add the sugar and vanilla extract; beat until light and fluffy. Add the eggs, one at a time, beating for 1 minute after each addition. Combine the flour, baking powder, and salt. Alternate adding the flour mixture with the cream of coconut and milk to the batter, beating on low speed after each addition until just combined. Spread the batter into the prepared pan.

3. Bake for about 25 minutes or until a wooden toothpick inserted in the center comes out clean. Cool thoroughly in the pan on a wire rack.

4. Once cool, cut the cake into three equal horizontal parts. These will create the layers. Set aside.

5. Prepare the custard: In a medium bowl, combine the pudding, coconut, and oil. Stir with a small rubber spatula until well mixed.

6. Prepare the icing: Beat the cream cheese, butter, and vanilla with an electric mixer until light and fluffy. Gradually add the confectioners' sugar, beating well.

7. To assemble the cake: Place the first layer on a parchment-lined rectangular baking dish. Divide the coconut custard filling in half and spread the first half over the bottom cake layer. Top with the second layer and cover with the rest of the filling. Top with the last layer and frost with the cream cheese icing. Top with large shreds of fresh coconut. Refrigerate for 1 hour until set.

Serves 8 to 10

Simplify: Purchase a prepared pound cake and premade vanilla pudding from the dairy case to assemble this cake without baking.

pistachio biscuits

½   cup (1 stick) unsalted butter, softened
½   cup sugar
1   large egg
1   tablespoon vanilla extract
¾   cup all-purpose flour
1   teaspoon baking powder
¾   cup coarsely chopped pistachios

1. In a medium bowl, beat the butter and sugar with an electric mixer on high speed until creamy. Add the egg and continue beating until combined. Add the vanilla extract and stir until smooth. Sift the flour with the baking powder; fold into the batter with the pistachios to form a stiff dough.

2. Turn the dough out onto a generously floured board and knead for 30 seconds. Divide the dough in half and shape into 2 logs, each 2 inches in diameter. Wrap the logs in plastic wrap and refrigerate for 30 minutes.

3. Preheat the oven to 350°F. Line a baking sheet with parchment paper or a silicone baking mat.

4. Using a sharp chef's knife, slice the logs of dough into ¼-inch thick slices and place on the prepared baking sheet. Bake for 8 to 10 minutes, until the cookies are golden brown. Using a metal spatula, transfer the cookies from the baking sheet to a wire rack to cool.

Makes 24 cookies

Simplify: Mix chopped pistachios with ready-made sugar cookie dough. Shape, refrigerate, slice, and bake as directed on the package.

braided cookies

Pair these simple, attractive biscuits with coffee or hot chocolate—they're light on sugar and pleasantly crisp and crunchy.

2	cups (4 sticks) unsalted butter
5	large eggs
1	cup sugar
1	tablespoon vanilla extract
5½	cups all-purpose flour, plus more, if needed
3	tablespoons baking powder
½	teaspoon salt
¼	cup sesame seeds

1. Preheat the oven to 350°F. Grease 2 baking sheets.

2. In a large mixing bowl, beat the butter with an electric mixer on high speed until light and fluffy. Add the sugar and beat for 10 minutes more on medium speed. Add 4 of the eggs, one at a time, beating well after each addition. Beat in the vanilla extract. In a medium bowl, whisk together the flour, baking powder, and salt. Add the flour mixture to the butter mixture and mix on low to form a soft, cohesive dough. Add a bit more flour if the dough is too soft to handle easily.

3. Lightly flour a work surface. Break off 1-inch pieces of dough and roll into ropes about 7 inches long and ¼ inch in diameter. Cross the ends of each rope to form a loop and twirl the loop in the opposite direction, forming a braid. Place the braids on the prepared baking sheets about 1 inch apart.

4. In a small bowl, beat the remaining egg. Using a pastry brush, brush the egg onto the braids; sprinkle with sesame seeds. Bake for 20 to 25 minutes until the cookies are golden brown. Cool on baking sheets for 10 minutes, then transfer to wire racks to cool completely.

Makes 24 cookies

Simplify: Greek markets and bakeries often sell these cookies. Purchase and keep fresh in an airtight container until ready to serve.

butter almond sticks

Rich, buttery, and crunchy with almonds—
irresistible.

1	cup (2 sticks) unsalted butter, softened
1	cup sugar
3	large eggs
1	teaspoon almond extract
3	cups all-purpose flour
¼	teaspoon salt
1½	cups finely chopped almonds

1. Preheat the oven to 350°F.

2. In a medium bowl, cream together the butter and ½ cup of the sugar until smooth. Stir in 1 of the eggs and the almond extract. In another medium bowl, whisk together the flour and salt; stir into the sugar mixture. Add the almonds and mix with your hands until combined and the dough has a sheen.

3. In a separate medium bowl, beat the remaining 2 eggs. Place the remaining ½ cup sugar in a small bowl. Lightly flour a work surface. Pinch off small pieces of dough and roll into ropes 2 to 3 inches long and ½-inch in diameter. Dip each rope first in the beaten eggs and then in the sugar. Place 1 inch apart on ungreased baking sheets. Bake for 8 to 10 minutes, just until the cookies begin to brown. Cool the cookies on the baking sheets for 5 minutes, then transfer to wire racks to cool completely.

Makes 24 cookies

Simplify: Purchase almonds that are already chopped.

brown sugar sandies

These treats owe their glistening, sparkly surface to a dusting of sanding sugar added when they are still hot. You'll find sanding sugar sold with cake decorating supplies; it comes in many colors.

2	cups brown sugar
1	cup molasses
1	cup plus 1 tablespoon vegetable shortening
2	large eggs
1	teaspoon ground cinnamon
1	teaspoon ground nutmeg
1	teaspoon ground cloves
5	teaspoons baking soda
½	cup water
2	cups all-purpose flour, more if needed
	Gold sanding sugar, for dusting

1. In a medium bowl, using a wooden spoon, blend together the brown sugar, molasses, and shortening until smooth. In a small bowl, beat the eggs. Add the cinnamon, nutmeg, and cloves to the sugar mixture and beat until just mixed. Add the egg mixture to the brown sugar mixture and stir until combined. Dissolve the baking soda in the water; stir into the brown sugar mixture. Gradually stir the flour into the brown sugar mixture, mixing until combined and the dough is stiff enough to roll out. Shape the dough into a ball; wrap in plastic wrap and refrigerate for 1 hour.

2. Preheat the oven to 350°F.

3. Lightly flour a work surface. Roll out the dough to ½-inch thickness. Using a sharp knife, cut the dough into 2 x 3-inch rectangles. Place the cookies ½ inch apart on ungreased baking sheets. Bake for 10 to 12 minutes, just until the cookies begin to brown. Remove from the oven and immediately sprinkle the cookies with sanding sugar. Transfer the cookies to wire racks to cool.

Makes 36 cookies

Simplify: Make a double batch and freeze the dough so you can make cookies when company drops by. Shape the dough into logs, wrap in plastic wrap, and refrigerate or freeze. When ready to bake, cut the logs into ½-inch slices.

chocolate cupcakes with peanut butter filling

These decadent-looking cupcakes are easy to make and more tempting with fresh chocolate ganache.

⅓	cup unsweetened cocoa powder
1½	cups all-purpose flour
1½	cups sugar
1½	teaspoons baking soda
½	teaspoon baking powder
½	teaspoon salt
2	large eggs
¾	cup water
¾	cup buttermilk
3	tablespoons vegetable oil
1	teaspoon vanilla extract
1½	cups creamy peanut butter
	Chocolate Ganache (page 142)

1. Preheat the oven to 350°F. Place liners in two standard 12-cup muffin tins.

2. In a large bowl, whisk together the cocoa powder, flour, sugar, baking soda, baking powder, and salt until combined. Whisk in the eggs, water, buttermilk, oil, and vanilla. Continue whisking until the batter is completely mixed.

3. Fill each muffin cup with ¼ cup batter. Bake 15 to 17 minutes, until a toothpick inserted into the center of a cupcake comes out clean. Cool the cupcakes in pans on wire racks for 10 minutes; then remove from the muffin pans. Cool completely before filling and icing.

4. Fit a pastry bag with a number 20 (small) star tip. Spoon the peanut butter into the bag. Press the tip into the center of a cupcake top; squeeze the bag for 3 seconds to fill the cupcake with about ¾ tablespoon peanut butter. Repeat for each cupcake. Set the bag aside.

5. Using a small knife, remove any excess peanut butter from the cupcake tops. Using an offset spatula, spread ganache over the top of each. Add a flourish to the top by squeezing a bit of peanut butter through the star tip.

Makes 24 cupcakes

Simplify: Begin with cupcakes from your favorite bakery—all you'll have to do is fill them with peanut butter and frost.

tiramisu

This is an easy dessert that can be assembled in individual serving dishes. It's very rich, so I serve it with two spoons for sharing.

1¼	cups mascarpone cheese
1½	cups heavy cream
3	tablespoons confectioners' sugar, sifted
½	cup strong espresso
½	cup coffee liqueur
1	cup prepared vanilla pudding
16	ladyfinger cookies, broken into pieces
	Unsweetened cocoa powder, for dusting

1. In a medium bowl, whisk together the mascarpone, cream, and confectioners' sugar until light and creamy. Set aside. In a small bowl, stir together the espresso and liqueur.

2. Spoon some pudding into a serving bowl or four glass tumblers. Top with pieces of ladyfinger and pour in enough espresso mixture to moisten the cookies. Spoon on a layer of the mascarpone mixture. Repeat the layering until the bowl is full. Dust heavily with cocoa powder and refrigerate until ready to serve.

Serves 4

Simplify: Purchase tiramisu-flavored mascarpone cheese to cut your prep time almost in half.

marshmallow espresso

Use handmade marshmallows to give this drink a fun but sophisticated twist. They have fresh, delicious flavor far superior to the packaged variety. Look for them at specialty food shops.

Hot espresso
Large marshmallows

For each serving, fill a votive cup with the coffee. Add a marshmallow and let it melt for 30 seconds; then serve immediately.

Simplify: It doesn't get any easier, but if you don't have an espresso machine, brew a bold, dark roast coffee in your regular coffeemaker or French press.

chocolate latte

The mix of coffee and chocolate flavors creates a drink rich like hot chocolate but with a roasted coffee kick.

1½	**cups half-and-half**
2	**tablespoons brown sugar**
2	**cups strong coffee or espresso**
¼	**cup chocolate syrup**
1	**teaspoon vanilla extract**
1	**cup frothed whole milk**
¼	**cup whiskey (optional)**
	Prepared caramel sauce, for serving

Heat the half-and-half in a saucepan over medium-high heat. (Do not boil.) Remove from the heat and stir in the brown sugar, coffee, chocolate syrup, vanilla extract, and whiskey. Pour into glass mugs and top with frothed milk. Top with a drizzle of the prepared caramel sauce.

Serves 4

holiday open house

It's the eternal holiday dilemma: You want to celebrate with family and friends, but who wants to add any more projects during this frenzied season? An open house with a buffet meal of easy, make-ahead foods can be the perfect solution. It's festive and elegant, but not exhausting. Buy whatever you don't have time to make.

menu
BISCUIT-TOPPED TURKEY POTPIE

SAUTÉED STRING BEANS

ULTIMATE CHOCOLATE TART

PUMPKIN TRIFLE

RASPBERRY-LIME PUNCH

POMEGRANATE-CHAMPAGNE COCKTAIL

Invite guests to help trim the tree or exchange gifts to get the party started. Rich, deep reds, soft gray-greens, and touches of gold and silver create a sophisticated variation on the typical red-and-green theme. Decorations look lush but are surprisingly simple: Place a mix of reddish fruits—such as apples, pomegranates, grapes and champagne grapes—in the glass cylinder. Add water and tuck in red roses and berries. For an unexpected centerpiece, stack the compote on top of the cake stand and fill with small wrapped gifts, ribbon-tied pouches, and mini red, gold, and green Christmas balls.

the recipes

Individual potpies cooked in oval bowls are easy to serve on the buffet table.

biscuit-topped turkey potpie

This meal is a satisfying update on a classic, and feeds a small crowd well. The filling is abundant, so be sure to bake this in ovenproof bowls or a large casserole that will hold it all.

FILLING

½	cup (1 stick) unsalted butter
2	carrots, peeled and cut into ½-inch pieces (1 cup)
2	stalks celery, cut into ½-inch pieces (1 cup)
½	cup chopped onion
½	cup frozen peas
3	tablespoons minced fresh parsley
1	teaspoon minced fresh thyme or ½ teaspoon dried thyme, crushed
½	teaspoon salt
½	teaspoon freshly ground black pepper
2½	cups chicken broth
1	bay leaf
12	ounces skinless, boneless turkey breasts or thighs
2	medium potatoes, peeled and chopped (1½ cups)
⅔	cup all-purpose flour
2	teaspoons fresh sage or 1 teaspoon dried sage, crushed
½	teaspoon dry mustard
1½	cups milk
2	tablespoons dry sherry

BISCUIT TOPPING

2¼	cups all-purpose flour
¾	cup sifted cake flour
4	teaspoons baking powder
¾	teaspoon baking soda
¾	teaspoon salt
1	tablespoon minced fresh parsley (optional)
1	tablespoon minced fresh rosemary (optional)
2	teaspoons minced fresh thyme (optional)
5	tablespoons cold unsalted butter
5	tablespoons vegetable shortening
1½	cups buttermilk, plus more for brushing (optional)

1. Prepare the filling: In a large skillet over medium heat, melt 3 tablespoons of the butter. Add the carrots, celery, and onion and cook, stirring, until tender, about 3 to 4 minutes. Stir in the peas, parsley, thyme, salt, and pepper and cook, stirring, for 1 minute more. Remove the pan from the heat; set aside.

2. In a large saucepan bring the broth and bay leaf to boiling over high heat; add the turkey. Cover the pan, reduce the heat, and simmer for 15 minutes or until the turkey is no longer pink, adding the potatoes for the last 7 minutes. Strain the broth and reserve; discard the bay leaf. Set the turkey and vegetables aside; when cool, chop the turkey into bite-size pieces.

3. In the same large saucepan over medium heat, melt the remaining 5 tablespoons of butter. Stir in the flour, sage, and mustard until combined and cook, stirring, until lightly browned, about 1 minute. Whisk in the reserved turkey broth and the milk. Cook, stirring, until the mixture is thick and bubbly, about 2 to 3 minutes. Remove the pan from the heat; stir in the sherry. Stir in the reserved turkey and vegetables. Cover and keep warm.

4. Preheat the oven to 400°F. Butter 8 ovenproof bowls (or a 3-quart casserole).

5. Prepare the biscuit topping: In a large mixing bowl or food processor, combine the flours, baking powder, baking soda, and salt. Add the parsley, rosemary, and thyme, if using. Sift the mixture three times (or pulse in the food processor). Using a pastry blender or two knives (or the blade attachment of the food processor), cut the butter and shortening into the dry ingredients until the pieces are pea-size. Add the buttermilk all at once, stirring or pulsing just until combined and a dough forms.

6. Pour the turkey mixture into the prepared bowls or casserole. Using a large spoon, drop the dough in 8 mounds on top of the turkey mixture. If desired, brush the mounds with additional buttermilk. Bake for 30 to 35 minutes or until the biscuit tops are golden and a wooden toothpick inserted near the center of one comes out clean.

Serves 8

Simplify: Use a precooked rotisserie turkey or chicken breast cut into bite-size pieces, frozen vegetables, and/or a packaged biscuit mix.

sautéed string beans

These green beans are a classic and delicious side dish. Serve them from a pretty casserole or in individual bowls.

1	tablespoon olive oil
4	cloves garlic, minced
1	pound fresh green beans, trimmed and snapped into 1-inch pieces
½	cup chicken broth
¼	teaspoon garlic salt
¼	teaspoon freshly ground black pepper

In a large skillet over medium heat, heat the oil. Add the garlic and cook, stirring, for 30 seconds. Stir in the green beans. Cover and cook, stirring occasionally, for 5 minutes more. Add the chicken broth; bring to boiling over high heat. Reduce the heat to medium, cover the skillet and cook until the beans are tender, 5 to 7 minutes more. Season with the garlic salt and pepper.

Serves 6 to 8

Simplify: Szechuan restaurants offer these beans for takeout; order in advance and gently reheat in the microwave for 2 minutes.

ultimate chocolate tart

This glorious chocolate dessert is like an oversize truffle. Serve it on a cake stand to give a flourish to your dessert table.

9	(1-ounce) squares bittersweet chocolate
1	cup all-purpose flour
4	teaspoons unsweetened cocoa powder, plus more for dusting
⅛	teaspoon salt
4	tablespoons (½ stick) unsalted butter, softened
¼	cup sugar
3	large eggs
1¼	cups heavy cream
¼	cup whole milk
⅓	cup superfine sugar
½	teaspoon vanilla extract

1. Chop and then melt 1 square of the chocolate and set aside to cool slightly. Chop the remaining 8 squares chocolate and set aside.

2. In a small bowl, stir together the flour, 4 teaspoons cocoa powder and salt; set aside. In a large bowl, using an electric mixer on medium speed, beat the butter and sugar until well combined. Beat in 1 of the eggs and the melted chocolate. Beat in the flour mixture until just combined. Cover the pastry with plastic wrap and refrigerate for 30 minutes or until easy to handle.

3. Preheat the oven to 400°F.

4. Press the pastry evenly onto the bottom and up the sides of a 9-inch tart pan with a removable bottom. Prick the bottom of the pastry shell with a fork, then line the shell with a double thickness of foil. Bake for 8 minutes. Remove the foil and bake 5 to 6 minutes more or until the shell is firm and dry.

5. Meanwhile, melt the remaining 8 squares chopped chocolate; set aside to cool slightly. When the pie shell is ready, transfer it to a wire rack to cool. Reduce the oven temperature to 350°F.

6. Using a pastry brush, brush about 3 tablespoons of the melted chocolate over the bottom of the prepared crust. Set aside.

7. In a medium saucepan over high heat, bring the cream and milk just to boiling. Gradually add the remaining melted chocolate, whisking until smooth. Remove the pan from the heat. In a small bowl, whisk together the remaining 2 eggs, superfine sugar, and vanilla. Whisk in about ½ cup cream mixture. Add the egg mixture to the cream mixture; stir until well combined.

8. Place the tart shell on a baking sheet on the middle oven rack. Carefully pour the filling into the tart shell (the shell will be full). Bake for 25 to 30 minutes or until the top is set when gently shaken and the filling is bubbly under the surface. Transfer the tart to a wire rack to cool completely. Before serving, dust with cocoa powder.

Serves 10 to 12

Make-ahead tip: Prepare the tart as directed, omitting the cocoa powder dusting. Cover and refrigerate up to 3 days. To serve, let the tart stand at room temperature 30 minutes; then dust with cocoa powder.

Simplify: Use a ready-made chocolate tart shell instead of making your own.

pumpkin trifle

This easy-to-assemble dessert can be put together by even the youngest member of your family and will be the hit of the party. Make individual servings or use one large compote or dish.

- ½   pint heavy cream
- ½   cup sugar
- 1   loaf pumpkin bread, cut into ½-inch thick slices
- 1   (10-ounce) jar pumpkin butter
- 1   cup bottled caramel sauce
- 2   cups prepared vanilla pudding
- ½   cup finely chopped walnuts or pecans

In a medium bowl, using an electric mixer on medium speed, whip the cream with the sugar until stiff. Arrange the remaining ingredients except for the nuts in layers in your chosen serving dish: Start with whipped cream, add some pumpkin bread (cut slices into smaller pieces if too large for individual dishes), spoon on some pumpkin butter, drizzle with caramel sauce, spoon on some vanilla pudding. Repeat this sequence, ending with whipped cream, until all the ingredients are used. Top with the nuts. Refrigerate until chilled, at least 30 minutes.

Serves 8

Simplify: If you can't find pumpkin bread, substitute cranberry-nut bread, pound cake, or gingerbread.

Make individual pumpkin trifles in bowls for a taste of the season.

raspberry-lime punch

A punch is a festive, easy way to serve a special drink to a large crowd without a lot of fuss.

1	(6-ounce) can frozen pineapple-orange juice concentrate, thawed
2	cups water
2	cups raspberry-blend fruit juice, chilled
½	cup lime juice
2	tablespoons sugar
2	liters lemon-lime soda, chilled
24	ice cubes
1	lime, thinly sliced
2	cups fresh or frozen raspberries

In a large punch bowl, stir together the pineapple-orange juice concentrate, water, raspberry juice, lime juice, and sugar. Stir until the sugar is dissolved. Slowly pour the lemon-lime carbonated beverage down the side of the bowl. Add the ice cubes. Float the lime slices and raspberries on top of the punch.

Makes 14 eight-ounce servings

Simplify: Mix everything except the soda, ice cubes, and raspberries ahead of time; refrigerate until the party, then complete the recipe.

pomegranate-champagne cocktail

Add some extra color and flavor to champagne with a shot of pomegranate juice. Have everything chilled and mix the following for each guest:

2   **tablespoons pomegranate juice or cranberry juice**
6   **tablespoons Champagne**

Measure the pomegranate juice into a Champagne flute. Slowly add Champagne. Serve immediately.

Serves 1

4
shortcuts, tips, and sources

stocking the bar

It is helpful to set up a bar not only for parties and special occasions, but also to keep drink ingredients on hand for last-minute entertaining.

The Basic Bar:
• Vodka
• Gin
• Light rum
• Bourbon
• Tequila
• Scotch
• Dry and sweet vermouth
• Angostura bitters
• Cointreau or Triple Sec
• White wine
• Red wine
• Beer: domestic, imported, and/or light

Mixers:
• Tonic water
• Seltzer or club soda
• Sparkling water
• Ginger ale
• Regular and diet colas and lemon sodas
• Orange juice, cranberry juice

party planning guidelines

• Have enough glasses and beverages on hand for guests to enjoy one drink an hour, or an average of three drinks per guest.

• Most standard drinks call for 1½ ounces of liquor, which means that you can make about 22 drinks from one liter of alcohol.

• A 750-milliliter bottle of wine holds 5 five-ounce servings of wine. A liter bottle holds ten glasses. A bottle of Champagne serves 6 four-ounce servings.

• You will need a liter of mixers (seltzer or club soda, tonic, sodas, juices) for every three guests.

• Allow a pound of ice per guest if you plan to have a full bar. This allows for cooling beverages and provides ice for drinks.

• An easier and less expensive alternative to stocking a full bar is to offer wine, beer, and a "signature" cocktail such as rum punch, margaritas, or cosmopolitans.

• For a dinner party, plan on one bottle (750 milliliter) of wine for every two people, unless you know your guests are big wine drinkers.

• For a crowd that's primarily beer drinkers, allow one six-pack for every two people, based on a 12-ounce serving.

• It's always considerate to serve some delicious nonalcoholic beverages as well, whether it's sparkling cider, lemonade, virgin daiquiris, Virgin Marys, or nonalcoholic wine or beer.

• Don't forget pitted green olives and lemon and lime slices for garnishing cocktails. Consider fresh berries and herbs like mint and lavender to take your drinks to the next level.

• Most liquors will keep for a long time, except vermouth, which is actually a wine and should be refrigerated and used fairly quickly.

last-minute entertaining

It is important to keep key ingredients stocked for spontaneous get-togethers. You should always have the elements to make a quick cheese and hors d'oeuvres plate or small bites like country ham and biscuits or turkey slivers on tea bread, as well as various drinks and punches. Having the basics for a dessert tray is also a good idea, so keep stocked with jam and whipped cream to sauce a frozen pound cake, cheesecake, or a trifle. Frozen cookies can be baked in minutes to accompany coffee and tea.

Keep the following items on hand, especially during the holidays, and you will always be prepared to entertain drop-in guests.

• In the cupboard: several types of crackers and crisp breads to accompany breads and cheeses, canned Mandarin oranges (to top cake or add to trifles), and jam, coffee, and tea.

• In the refrigerator: semisoft cheese, hard cheese, dip, and salsa. Two bottles of white wine, ginger ale, cranberry juice, seltzer, lemons and limes, and whipping cream. At holiday time, consider a spiral-sliced ham or smoked turkey breast.

• In the freezer: fruit bread, biscuits, cheesecake, pound cake, frozen cookie dough.

• In the entertaining pantry: red wine; taper, pillar, and votive candles.

linen care and storage

Clean and store your linens properly so you're always ready for an event.

• Clean and launder all fabrics prior to storing. Freshly iron and starch a day or two prior to the event.

• Fold or roll items around a cardboard fabric roll or mailing tube and store them in a cool, dry, and well-ventilated area.

• A professional laundry or dry cleaner can launder and press your linens. Ask items to be folded and placed on a hanger. Before use, iron to remove deep folds and wrinkles.

• Don't store linens in plastic; they need to breathe. You can protect linens by storing them in old cotton pillowcases, if needed.

how to clean glassware

• Use a plastic dishwashing basin or line the bottom of your sink with a rubber mat or towel. Fill with hot soapy water. (Add a little ammonia to cut grease if needed.) Slowly slide stemware into the water, holding the glass by the bowl, not the stem. Swish around with a dishcloth and then rinse in clear hot or warm water (cool water could shatter the glass).

• For clear, streak-free glasses, add a little white vinegar or borax to the final rinse water.

• Dry glasses upside down on a cotton towel or dry carefully with a tea towel.

• Never place crystal in the dishwasher. The high, prolonged heat can cause it to break, and the detergent can etch and dull the surface. Always hand wash.

• Do not wash delicate, hand-painted, gold- or silver-rimmed glasses or dinnerware in the dishwasher.

• If two glasses are stuck together, fill the inner glass with ice water and dip the outer glass in a bowl of warm water. Gradually increase the temperature of the warm water until the outer glass expands and the two glasses can be gently separated.

caring for silver and stainless flatware

• Rinse salt and acidic foods (tomatoes, vinegar, wine) off silverware, glazed dinnerware, and crystal as soon as possible.

• To restore a large batch of tarnished silver, try this method: Mix a solution of 5 ounces dry milk powder, 12 ounces water, and 1 tablespoon white vinegar. Pour in a 9 x 13-inch baking pan. Add tarnished silverware and let sit overnight. Rinse and dry pieces thoroughly.

• Store silver in bags or cases made from tarnish-resistant cloth such as Pacific cloth.

• Place one or two pieces of white chalk in your silverware chest to prevent tarnishing.

• Do not allow stainless-steel flatware to touch silver in the dishwasher. It can pit the stainless surface and leave black spots. It is preferable to wash silver by hand.

the fun art of napkin folding

Add style to your table with creatively folded napkins. For lots of classic and clever ideas and step-by-step instructions, visit www.napkinfoldingguide.com.

candle tips

I prefer to use fragrance-free, dripless candles for the best results and easiest clean up. Here are some tips to get the most from your candles:

• Always cut the wick of the candle to ¼-inch before lighting, both for safety and to prevent the wick from smoking or crumbling into the wax.

• Allow candles in a container to burn long enough so that the hot wax extends to all sides. This will ensure that the candle burns down evenly, maximizing its burn time.

• Keep candles away from drafts or breezy windows. Drafty areas will cause the candle to burn unevenly, or it could be knocked over and start a fire.

• To remove melted wax from candlesticks or votive holders:

  • Once the candle has burned within two inches of the bottom, snuff the wick and allow the wax to become solid.

  • If the candle can't be removed easily, place the candleholder in the freezer, upside down if possible, for 10 to 15 minutes. Take it out, give it a little smack on the bottom, and the candle should pop right out.

  • If the candle does not pop out or you have waited a long time to remove the wax, take a butter knife and cut into the candle in a straight line. Before you have gotten halfway down, the candle should pop out.

• To make votive or tea light candles easy to remove, place ¼-inch of water in the holder so the melted wax or candle will come out with the water.

• Refrigerate candles for an hour or two before your event to help them burn more slowly and evenly. (Note: Refrigerating them for too long can cause them to crack.)

• Placing candles close to one another will affect how quickly and evenly they burn due to their combined heat. As a rule of thumb, place candles at least 3 inches apart.

• Candles should be stored flat. This is particularly true of long taper candles, which tend to bend. Store candles in a place that stays cool and dark year-round. Temperatures above 70°F for prolonged periods of time can soften candles. If they are not lying flat and not wrapped individually, candles run the risk of bending or melting together at high temperatures. If wrapped and stored properly, candles should be able to withstand summertime temperatures.

• Anchor taper candles securely and help them stand tall by placing sticky wax buttons (often available where candles are sold) in the bottom of candlesticks. Or, try wrapping aluminum foil around the base of the candle to create a tighter fit.

• Pillar candles should be placed on platters, plates, or saucers to create a sturdy base and catch any drips.

special sources

PANTRY CUPBOARDS, SHELVES, CARTS, AND CUBES

IKEA
www.ikea.com/us
Well-priced shelving units, cupboards and storage options.

Pottery Barn
www.potterybarn.com
A wide range of well-priced and attractively styled wooden shelves, storage units, and armoires.

West Elm
www.westelm.com
This younger, more modern, even more affordable sibling of Pottery Barn offers intriguing shelves, storage cubes, and modular storage units.

Crate & Barrel
www.crateandbarrel.com
An extensive collection of well-designed storage cubes, stacking shelves, and bookcases.

CB2
www.cb2.com
Like West Elm, this is the hipper, cheaper version of Crate & Barrel. Sleek shelves, storage units, and bookcases.

Design Within Reach
www.dwr.com
Innovative, sleekly designed modern storage including modular units, cubes, and shelves.

DISHES, GLASSES, FLATWARE, AND SERVING PIECES

IKEA
www.ikea.com
Extremely affordable stoneware and glass tableware, in simple, clean-lined shapes.

Crate & Barrel
www.crateandbarrel.com
Virtually everything for the table and entertaining: dinnerware, flatware, glasses, candleholders, platters, and appetizer plates.

Pottery Barn
www.potterybarn.com
A wide range of dishes, glassware, flatware, linens, and serving pieces, with a pretty collection of creamy white cake stands, pitchers, and platters.

West Elm
www.westelm.com
Simple, modern dinnerware.

Williams-Sonoma
www.williams-sonoma.com
A comprehensive yet well-edited selection of dinnerware, cookware, glassware, and serving pieces, including cake stands, platters, and pitchers.

Target
www.target.com
This well-priced accessible retailer specializes in good design at great prices. They sell the basics as well as unexpectedly sophisticated fare including condiment dishes and footed glass bowls. Their designer collections often sell out quickly, but are worth seeking out. Their website allows you to shop for tableware by color, a useful feature.

Pillivuyt
www.pillivuytus.com
High-quality white porcelain tableware from France in timeless designs. Available through specialty retailers.

Wedgwood
www.wedgwoodusa.com
This fine-quality English china company
is known for its white bone china in
designs ranging from sophisticated
minimalism to traditional elegance.

Pearl River Mart
www.pearlriver.com
477 Broadway
New York, NY 10013
800-878-2446
This Chinatown store offers an
incredible array of Asian imports,
including an extensive collection of
simple white porcelain restaurant ware,
as well as colorful paper goods, all at
irresistible prices.

Fishs Eddy
www.fishseddy.com
889 Broadway at 19th Street
New York, NY 10003
212-420-9020
These stores began selling vintage
dinnerware and remaindered patterns,
but now also offer their own range
of sturdy ironstone and commercial
dinnerware, including their "Diner
White" collection, at very affordable
prices.

Sur La Table
www.surlatable.com
800-243-0852
These stores across the country offer
gourmet cookware, a wide selection
of European-inspired dinnerware, and
an impressive array of serving pieces,
from eggcups to glass cloches, ceramic
baking dishes to cake stands.

Broadway Panhandler
www.broadwaypanhandler.com
65 East 8th Street
New York, NY 10003
866-266-5927
Best known for their professional
selection of cookware, this store also
offers some serving pieces, such as
milk glass cake stands.

Linens-N-Things
www.lnt.com
One of the country's largest
housewares retailers, these big-box
stores offer well-priced tableware and
serving pieces in simple white and
glass patterns, as well as white table
linens.

Home Goods
www.homegoods.com
Nationwide stores that offer a changing
selection of tableware and home
accessories at a 20 to 60 percent
discount.

**STORES AND ONLINE PURVEYORS
OF GOURMET FOODS**

Whole Foods
www.wholefoods.com
An upscale grocery chain specializing
in natural and organic foods, with many
gourmet, hard-to-find ingredients
and delicious ready-made foods, from
appetizers to desserts.

Wegmans Food Markets
www.wegmans.com
A sophisticated grocery store offering
quality fresh foods, international finds,
and gourmet prepared foods.

Trader Joe's
www.traderjoes.com
This friendly national chain features
natural and organic foods, as well as
tasty frozen prepared foods, all at
exceptional prices.

Eli's Manhattan
www.elizabar.com
1411 Third Avenue
New York, NY 10028
212-717-8100
This New York City gem offers delicious
hearth-baked breads and unique
pantry staples.

Dean & DeLuca
www.deandeluca.com
New York, NY
Founded in Soho in the 1970s, Dean &
DeLuca still is the preeminent gourmet
grocery, featuring epicurean and
artisanal foods from around the world,
all beautifully displayed. The store
also offers a limited but sophisticated
selection of white tableware,
including Pillivuyt, and coffee and tea
accoutrements.

Formaggio Kitchen
www.formaggiokitchen.com
244 Huron Avenue
Cambridge, MA 02137
617-354-4750
This Boston-based gourmet shop
features international artisanal
cheeses, handmade sweets, and hard-
to-find spices and salts.

La Grande Epicerie de Paris
www.lagrandeepicerie.fr/index_en.asp
22 Rue de Sevres
Paris, France 75007
01 44 39 81 20
This wonderful Parisian grocery store,
located in Le Bon Marché on the Left
Bank, has an exquisite selection of
products from around the world. If
you're lucky enough to go to Paris, this
is a must-see shop.

Foster's Market
www.fostersmarket.com
2694 Chapel Hill Road
Durham, NC 27707
and
750 Martin Luther King Jr. Blvd.
Chapel Hill, NC 27514
Renowned chef and cookbook author
Sara Foster's upscale markets include
a café, specialty grocery store, and
catering business, all featuring her
casual southern flair.

L'Epicerie
www.lepicerie.com
L'Epicerie offers the kind of fine-quality
and hard-to-find ingredients only chefs
and bakers usually have access to, in
quantities for the home cook. Their
European-inspired website offers
excellent fruit purées, preserves,
ready-to-bake croissants, condiments,
spices, as well as kitchenware.

Melissa's
www.melissas.com
Exotic, organic, and specialty fruits
and vegetables, delivered to your door
farm-fresh.

The Spice House
www.thespicehouse.com
An exhaustive array of premium-
quality, hard-to-find spices, herbs,
and rubs, including well-priced gift
samplers.

Lobel's of New York
www.lobels.com
This legendary Upper East Side butcher
offers USDA prime dry-aged steaks,
roasts, and specialty meats.

Legal Sea Foods
www.legalseafoods.com
The famous Boston seafood
restaurant, now franchised across the
country, offers fresh-caught lobsters
and fish through its website.

Harbor Candy Shop
www.harborcandy.com
This Ogunquit, Maine, chocolate shop
offers rich chocolates, handmade from
the freshest ingredients.

New Skete Kitchens
www.newskete.com/products.htm
You may have heard of the monks
of New Skete, who are famous for
training dogs, but the nuns of New
Skete, also located in upstate New
York, make nationally famous gourmet
cheesecakes to support their mission.

Ice Cream Source
www.icecreamsource.com
Nearly every brand and flavor of ice
cream you've ever heard of, plus some
you haven't.

**RIBBON, PAPER EMBELLISHMENTS,
RUBBER STAMPS, AND LABELS**

Michaels
www.michaels.com
This huge crafts department store,
with locations throughout the U.S. and
Canada, offers everything imaginable
for your projects—papers, scrapbook
embellishments, stickers, charms,
stationery supplies, and more.

A.C. Moore
www.acmoore.com
This national superstore features arts
and crafts supplies, floral supplies,
and an extensive line of scrapbooking,
stamping, and paper goods.

Mokuba
www.mokubany.com
55 West 39th St.
New York, NY 10018
212-869-8900
Gossamer, beautifully colored wire-
edged ribbons, and trims in every
imaginable shade and style are
showcased at this Japanese company's
large design center.

Tinsel Trading
www.tinseltrading.com
47 West 38th Street
New York, NY 10018
212-730-1030
Wonderful collection of vintage-style
trims, amazing ribbons, buttons, glass
glitter, millinery flowers, and more.

Kate's Paperie
www.katespaperie.com
Several locations, including:
72 Spring Street in Soho, between
Crosby and Lafayette
New York, NY 10012
212-941-9816
This is where paper and stationery
addicts feel like they've died and gone to
heaven. Beautiful and unusual papers, as
well as menu and place cards, scrapbook
embellishments, and more.

Midori
www.midoriribbon.com
708 6th Avenue North
Seattle, WA 98109
800-659-3049
Midori employs her Japanese heritage
and impeccable taste to create
gorgeous ribbons and handmade
papers, as well as favor boxes, bags,
and custom-printed ribbons.

Hyman Hendler & Sons
www.hymanhendler.com
67 West 38th Street
New York, NY 10018
212-840-8393
An old-fashioned purveyor of lavish
ribbons and trims.

Pearl Paint
www.pearlpaint.com
308 Canal Street
New York, NY 10013
212-431-7932
One of the best-known discount art
supply stores, with branches across
the country.

Flax Art & Design
www.flaxart.com
1699 Market Street
San Francisco, CA 94103
415-552-2355
A favorite haunt of artists, filled with
interesting papers, stationery, and art
supplies.

Bell'occhio
www.bellocchio.com
8 Brady Street
San Francisco, CA 94103
415-864-4048
A whimsical and winsome specialty
shop with a French accent, offering
unique curiosities, including cards, gift
tags, ribbons, and wrapping papers.

Print Icon
www.printicon.com
7 West 18th Street
New York, NY 10011
212-255-4489
Artisan-made papers, including vellum
and metallic papers, invitations, po-
chettes, as well as high-quality printing.

Target
www.target.com
This nationwide discount store
offers colorful, stylish invitations,
embellishments, and wrapping papers,
all at inexpensive prices.

Zimman's
www.zimmans.com
80 Market Street
Lynn, MA 01901
781-598-9432
A fabric and home decorating store with
an expansive line of decorative textiles
and trims from around the world.

Jo-Ann Fabrics
www.joann.com
This nationwide chain has everything for
your fabric, crafts, and sewing needs.

Calico Corners
www.calicocorners.com
These stores across the country
carry thousands of beautiful home
decorating fabrics and trims.

Tender Buttons
143 East 62nd Street
New York, NY 10021
212-758-7004
This shop is a goldmine for button lovers, with vintage and antique buttons as well as new ones in every style and material imaginable.

Gordon Button Co. Inc.
222 West 38th Street
New York, NY 10018
212-921-1684
A button company specializing in glittery, elegant styles at wholesale prices.

Britex Fabrics
www.britexfabrics.com
146 Geary Street
San Francisco, CA 94108
415-392-2910
One of the largest collections of fine fabrics and accessories under one roof.

FRESH FLOWERS AND HERBS

Flowerbud
www.flowerbud.com
877-524-5400
Premium, farm-fresh flowers in large quantities, shipped directly to your door.

Beyond Blossoms
www.beyondblossoms.com
Farm-fresh flowers, by the stem or in European hand-tied bouquets. Just place in a vase and you're done.

Gilbertie's Herb Gardens
www.gilbertiesherbs.com
7 Sylvan Lane
Westport, CT 06880
800-874-3727
Offering wonderful, hard-to-find herbs and herbal topiaries, in various shapes and species, for sale at their greenhouses. If you're within driving distance, it's worth the trip.

CAKE AND CANDY FLOWERS

Petit Fleurs
www.petitfleurs.com
41364 Paseo Padre Parkway
Fremont, CA 94539
510-651-1530
Fondant flowers and other edible cake decor. Custom orders welcome.

Candied Flowers by Meadowsweets
www.candiedflowers.com
173 Kramer Road
Middleburgh, NY 12122
888-827-6477
Their gorgeous farm-grown flowers are crystallized one at a time by hand, and include pansies, violas, daisies, and roses.

Fancy Flours
www.fancyflours.com
424 East Main Street, Suite 102b
Bozeman, MT 59715
406-522-8887
A great source for pastry decorating, including a wonderful selection of dragées, as well as sugar flowers, cookie cutters, and crystallized rose and violet petals.

Chandler's
www.chandlerscakeandcandy.com
7 Perley Street
Concord, NH 03301
603-223-0393
Cake and candy making supplies including hard-to-find candy molds, packaging, icing flowers, edible markers, and more.

index

Note: Page numbers in *italics* indicate pages with photos.

A

Alcoholic beverages. *See* Bar; Cocktail(s); Wine(s)
Almond(s), butter sticks, 150, *151*
Appetizers
 plates/bowls for, *14*, *53*, 68–69
 See also Hors d'oeuvres
Apple coffeecake, *52*, 64, *65*
Asparagus
 with herb-roasted chicken, 38, *39*
 salad with prosciutto, 54, *55*
Avocado
 and lobster salad, 100, *101*
 -tomato salsa, 120, *121*

B

Baking dishes
 multiple uses for, *26*
 as pantry item, 14
Bar
 garnishes, holders for, 44–45
 stocking for gatherings, 174Bar cart as pantry, 12
Barbecue, 74–89
 relaxed atmosphere for, *79*
 table setting for, *79*
Beef, herb-grilled tenderloin, 80, *81*
Berry(ies)
 and custard gallette, 46, *47*
 plum compote, 106, *107*
 trifle, quick, *49*
 and yogurt caramel, 60, *61*
Biscuit-topped turkey potpie, *162*, 163
Bottles, milk. *See* Glass milk bottles
Bowls
 basic, *16*
 mixing bowls, *19*
 oval, small, *18*, *162*
 for seafood tower, *117*
 See also specific type of bowl
Braided cookies, 148, *149*
Brandy, ginger pear popsicles, *119*, 130
Bread(s)
 cheese strata, 58, *59*
 as place card holders, 32, *37*
 rosemary, mini, 44, *45*
 tomato salad, *86*
Bread sticks, homemade, 50, *51*

Brioche rounds with goat cheese, honey, and figs, 126, *127*
Brown sugar
 glaze, 62
 sandies, 150, *151*
Brunch, lazy day gathering, 48–65
Buffet
 cake stand serving piece, *53*
 glass cylinder protector, *70*
 platters for organizing, *60*
Bundt cake, pumpkin, mini, *53*, 62, *63*
Butter almond sticks, 150, *151*

C

Cake(s)
 coconut, 144, *145*
 peach shortcake, 88, *89*
 pumpkin bundt cake, mini, 62, *63*
 shopping guide for, 187
 spicy ginger, 108, *109*
Cake stand
 multiple uses of, *23*, *53*, *55–57*, *72*, *161*, *184*
 personalizing, *89*
Candles
 citronella votives for barbecues, *79*
 eggcup holders for, *82*
 glass cylinder for, *71*
 glass voltive holders, *118*
 hors d'oeuvre bowls for, *76*
 ice bucket as holder, *90*, *181*
 tips for use, *180*
 types of, *20*, *114*
 various heights, 114, *115*
 wine glass holders, *48*
Caramel, mixed berries and yogurt, 60, *61*
Carrot(s)
 ginger soup, 56, *57*
 roasted root vegetables, 40, *41*
Carts. *See* Rolling cart
Celery vases, multiple uses of, *23*, *139*
Centerpiece, unexpected items for, *37*, *70*, *161*
Champagne, -pomegranate cocktail, *171*
Cheese
 course, ID tags, *66*
 goat, brioche rounds with honey, figs and, 126, *127*
 goat, herbed bites, *119*, 124
 strata, 58, *59*
 and tomato quiche, 102, *103*

Chicken, herb-roasted, 38, *39*
Children, as helpers, *31*
Chinese takeout, 66–73
 serving tips, 72–73
 suggested menu, 67
Chocolate
 cupcakes with peanut butter filling, 152, *153*
 -dipped spoons, *66–67*
 ganache, 142, *143*
 latte, *157*
 sandwich cookies, super rich, 142, *143*
 tart, ultimate, 166, *167*
 -topped ice cream cones, mini, 130, *131*
Cocktail(s)
 bar, stocking, 174
 lemonade, spiked, 132, *133*
 milk bottle for serving, 50–51
 pomegranate-champagne cocktail, *171*
 raspberry-lime punch, *170*
 sangria, fresh fruit, *87*
Cocktail party, 112–133
Coconut cake, 144, *145*
Coffee
 chocolate latte, *157*
 marshmallow espresso, *156*
Coffeecake, apple, 64, *65*
Coffee cup sleeves, 136, 140, *141*
Coffeehouse gathering, 134–157
 setting for, 136
Coffee pot
 multiple uses for, *26*
 as pantry item, 14
Compote
 berry plum, 106, *107*
 glass, multiple uses of, *23*, *47*, *72*, *136*, *161*
Cookies
 braided, 148, *149*
 brown sugar sandies, 150, *151*
 butter almond sticks, 150, *151*
 chocolate sandwich, super rich, 142, *143*
 pistachio biscuits, 146, *147*
Corn salad, 82, *83*
Countdown to event, tips for, 98
Cream cheese icing, 144
Cream/sugar
 eggcup servers, *53*
 milk bottle for serving, 50–51